SHRUBS

SHRUBS

J. R. B. Evison, OBE, NDH, VMH, FLS

OCTOPUS
BOOKS

Contents

First published in 1979

This edition published in 1985 by Octopus Books Limited
59 Grosvenor Street London W1

© 1979 Hennerwood Publications Limited

Reprinted 1986

ISBN 0 7064 2302 X

Printed in Hong Kong

Introduction

THERE are many thousands of different species and cultivars of shrubs on the market. Not unnaturally, every nurseryman does his best in his catalogue to make them sound equally desirable; but they simply cannot be. Some beautiful plants have so little vigour that they are nearly always a disappointment, or they produce glorious flowers so sparsely as to be scarcely worth having; others, although usefully hardy and vigorous in growth, are not really attractive enough to earn a place in the garden. A gardener who sees examples of the former which have won a high award at a flower show cannot know their drawbacks as far as vigour and bounty are concerned; while a catalogue emphasizing that the latter are strong and easy to grow will probably omit to mention their lack of beauty.

The Council of the Royal Horticultural Society recognized this problem as long ago as 1922 and instituted the Award of Garden Merit Scheme to identify plants of proved and outstanding excellence for garden use everywhere—plants which are, moreover, easy to obtain and easy to grow. Since then more than 1,000 plants have been honoured with this award. Not all are shrubs: annuals, herbaceous plants, bulbous plants, trees, rock garden plants, and water plants are included; but shrubs form the vast majority, and it is my intention to rely heavily on the Award of Garden Merit (AGM) list in this book. Readers can be confident that each of the AGM plants I mention is among the best of its type, and that if it does not do well it is unlikely to be the fault of the plant or the nurseryman. (One could not, for instance, expect an acid-loving rhododendron, however meritorious, to thrive if it was planted on the alkaline soil of the South Downs.)

Some very useful plants are not especially beautiful, and do not therefore qualify for the Award of Garden Merit but I have included a few of them for specific usages. Some very tough, protective plants for the seaside, and some good hedging plants, are of this kind.

The rose is possibly the most important group of shrubs. It is not dealt with here, because it is the subject of another book in this series. But do not let that deter you from using shrub roses and rose climbers among the other shrubs you may plant.

Botanical Names
A word about the styling of botanical names may be helpful. Plants most commonly have two names, both printed in italics: the first name denotes the genus and the second the species.

For instance, all lilacs belong to the genus *Syringa*; a particular species, for example the Korean lilac, is classified as *Syringa velutina*. Often a plant's name includes a third word, also in italics, as in *Syringa oblata giraldii*. This identifies a naturally occurring variety or subspecies—a form that differs from the species type, but not sufficiently to be classed as a separate species. A third name may appear not in italics but in quotation marks, as in *Syringa microphylla* 'Superba'. This means that the plant is not a natural variety but a cultivar (cultivated variety).

The other plant forms that appear frequently in this book are the hybrids, which are developed by cross-breeding two species of the same or different genera. These are identified either by an '×' between the genus and the species names – for instance, *Syringa × josiflexa* (the Rouen lilac) – or by the genus name followed only by a name in quotation marks, as in *Syringa* 'Ethel M. Webster'. To avoid confusion, a cultivar of a hybrid is identified by using the '×' form followed by the cultivar name in quotation marks, as in *Syringa × josiflexa* 'Bellicent'.

Shrubs contribute a remarkable variety of size, form, and colour to the garden scene. Here dwarf shrubs, climbers, conifers, and shrub roses blend attractively with other plants.

1 Setting the Scene

SHRUBS are plants which produce a number of woody shoots near their base, as distinct from trees, which develop a single trunk or bole before the shoots or branches appear. Their immense variety of flower and form makes shrubs the backbone of almost every garden. All too many small gardens are flat and regular in shape, so our first task is to give life and interest by introducing differing heights and shapes in the subjects we plant. This can be done more successfully with shrubs than with any other type of plant, so great is their variety of form and appearance.

Although trees as defined above have no place in this book, there are a few which are inclined to branch out so near to the ground that they may find a place among the shrubs and play the role of a tall corner-filler or a lawn specimen. Nearly every garden of any size has such a need for height for screening, privacy, or simply to improve the proportions of the garden. For years I had beside my front door a pink autumn-flowering cherry tree, whose branches had a habit of producing a flat tracery of branchlets which gave it a 'Japanese' appearance when covered with their light green foliage. This cherry started to flower in November and was frequently still blooming in March, and it gave me and hundreds of passers-by much pleasure. It has the somewhat elephantine Latin name of *Prunus subhirtella autumnalis rosea*. If you are thinking of buying one, insist on the *rosea* (pink) form, which is more attractive than the normal white. The strawberry tree, *Arbutus unedo*, is another bush-tree with several periods of beauty. Its branches twist and turn as it grows to give an appearance of age beyond its years, and the bark flakes off to reveal a delightful, smooth, cinnamon-coloured skin which lights up the winter scene. The strawberry tree is evergreen and the flowers come in the autumn in panicles of white pitcher-shaped bells. The fruits which give rise to its common name appear at the same time but are, of course, the slowly maturing product of the flowers of a year earlier. They hang in red clusters, are circular in shape, and are reminiscent of the strawberry only to the short-sighted. They are not inedible, but I know of no one who has taken a second bite! This arbutus has a child, *A. × andrachnoides*, which has all its parent's virtues but better bark colour, flower, and fruit. Additionally, it grows well on chalky soil, which is unusual for an ericaceous plant (that is, a member of the heath family).

If I were allowed to choose one more non-shrub, I might pick the Judas tree, *Cercis siliquastrum*. This is strictly a plant for the warmer parts of the country, coming as it does from southern Europe and the East, but if you give it a warm and well-drained spot it may give you much joy, even in a town garden. In May the Judas tree bears rosy purple, pea-shaped flowers, some directly out of the trunk and branches as well as on the flowering shoots. Soon after, the flat, almost circular leaves appear. Some say they resemble the money Judas took; others that he hanged himself on a tree of this species.

The changing garden scene

World War II changed many things in the gardening world, the main difference being in the size and complexity of the average garden. In both the large and the small garden the famous English herbaceous border was a casualty. It had become too specialized a subject to survive, fulfilling itself over too short a season to earn a place in the smaller garden and, in these days of acute labour shortage, absorbing too much of the available effort to retain its dominance in the larger garden.

The herbaceous border did not, however, disappear completely but merged with the old shrub border to become the popular mixed border. Gardeners today can be heard talking of their 'border' unaware that their mixture of shrubs, the best of the herbaceous plants, the larger bulbs such as the 'Summer Snowflake', and even the occasional space allotted to annuals, is quite a recent development.

It is no part of my brief to deal with plants other than shrubs, but I will just say that when you are choosing plants to go with your shrubs you should look for the same qualities as those found in the best shrubs. They must be distinctive in their own right, whether it be for shape, for flower, for contrast, or for some other quality — and probably for more than one. They must be hardy and add an interest to the border which is not already present.

The Killarney strawberry tree, *Arbutus unedo* Rubra', has an interesting shape, unique cinnamon bark, clusters of pitcher-shaped pink flowers, and strawberry-like fruits.

Planning the border

This is not a job to be undertaken in a hurry; it is essential to think the whole thing out before you begin to plant – or even to buy. One of the first things you have to decide on is the combination of shape and colour you want.

I find a mixture of grey with pink and mauve (as with, say, lavender, pink phlox or roses, and *Lilium regale*) quite charming, but there is no guarantee that you will think the same. So if you can spend a summer looking at other people's gardens and noting combinations which appeal to you, so much the better. How do you get into the gardens of strangers? Often you do not need to – they are in full view of all at the front. If you do not recognize a plant, you will find there is a marvellous freemasonry among gardeners; a polite enquiry will often yield far more than a pleasant answer.

Even more useful, perhaps, might be visits to the many gardens which are opened for charitable purposes, such as the Royal Gardeners' Benevolent Society or the National Garden Scheme. Booklets are available with details of where and when gardens are open and local libraries or newspapers often have information also. These gardens can be treasurehouses of ideas and you will have much enjoyment in seeking them out. There are also, of course, the gardens of the National Trust; of many famous Parks Departments; the Royal Botanic Gardens at Kew; and the Royal Horticultural Society's garden at Wisley, Surrey – probably the most widely interesting and extensively visited garden in Britain. When you visit the larger gardens be sure to keep in mind their proportions; you will be working on a much smaller scale.

Having gathered your ideas, you will then have to translate them into action. A plan drawn to scale will save

The potential of a shrub border is shown in this arrangement at Chelsea Flower Show. It includes Japanese maples, hydrangeas, azaleas, cornus, and others.

many a disappointment. You really do need to know what shape each group is to be and how many plants you need to achieve the desired effect. You will have noted in your garden viewing that good borders are not planted in formal blocks but rather in informal groupings, with the size of each group dependent on the dominance of particular plants. You will also find that odd numbers of plants – threes, fives, sevens – are easier to arrange attractively than even ones.

One of the easiest ways to produce a simple plan is to use squared paper. The width of the border should not be greater than that of the tallest plant you intend to use in it, so 2.5 m (8 ft) is a good width. Length is decided by the room available in the garden, say 10 m (33 ft). Mark these as a rectangle on your paper and then fill it in with your selected plants, putting, say, a red outline for shrubs, black for herbaceous plants, and green for bulbs. If your groupings look in proportion on paper, then I assure you they will also do so in the garden.

A mixed border of shrubs, perennials, and bulbs. Such arrangements of contrasting shapes and forms have largely replaced the herbaceous border.

2 Preparation

WHEREVER your garden may be, on whatever soil, you are likely to come up against problems of one sort or another. I am still waiting to find a friend who gardens on the easily worked medium loam all the good books tell us we should aim for! If your problem is intractable clay soil I can give you little comfort. Churchillian exhortations of 'blood, sweat, and tears' are not popular these days, but there is no doubt that hard work is just about the only answer if you want to correct the characteristic tendency of clay to coldness and consequent 'lateness'.

Drainage is a complicated art and one well worth taking professional advice about. It could also be one of the soundest investments in the clayey garden. Remember that water does not move laterally to any extent, but mainly downwards, so keep the drains shallow – 300 to 500 mm (1 to 1½ ft) deep – for the best results, and keep lateral drains close together, say at intervals of 3 m (10 ft). Make sure that the water has somewhere to drain to, even if you have to create a pond. Cover the drainpipes with shingle or something similar to prevent them becoming clogged with soil.

Preparing the soil

Clay is difficult to work owing to the extremely small size of the individual particles and because they tend to adhere to each other in a glutinous mass. Only by breaking this bond between the particles can clay be made more workable. The best ways of doing this are:
(1) Adding chalk or ground limestone at about 100 g/m² (4 oz/sq yd). This removes some stickiness, if only temporarily.
(2) Adding anything which will physically cause a break up of the clay mass. This will be of more per-

manent value. Compost, rotting straw, animal manures, and peat are a few of the natural things which can be dug in. They are especially useful in that they encourage an increase in the worm population. The benefit of worms in the soil is enormous, partly because they pass the soil directly through the gut as they move, making it friable, and partly be-

cause their working holes provide useful drainage passages.

Other gritty materials are sometimes also added to clay: coarse sand and grit, broken-brick fragments – in fact anything which will separate the sticky particles.

All these methods require a willingness to dig, that is, to turn over the soil to the depth of a spade's blade. Properly done, this means that the top 250 mm (10 in) is completely inverted. The compost or grit mentioned above should be worked in as digging continues. If you do this job in the autumn, the winter frosts will help to break the clay down.

Sandy soils, on the other hand, are made up of comparatively large soil particles and are very easy to dig. You can, moreover, do your digging whenever you want as they are rarely too wet to walk on. However, someone once described sand as 'the soil with the least backache and the most heartache': it may be a cultivator's dream and have the virtues of warmth and thus of earliness, but it contains little nutritious matter and does not resist drought well. It is therefore a good idea to dig compost, animal manure, or rotting straw into sandy soils to increase their food- and moisture-holding capacity.

You will need to supplement this with fertilizers, preferably those which

Above left A well-maintained shrub border. **Right** One of the best viburnums for smaller gardens, *V. × juddii* bears numerous, delightfully scented flowers in May.

give a slow, steady feed. Bone meal and hoof-and-horn are natural slow-release foods. There are also many excellent proprietary brands of 'complete' fertilizer which can be used for spring dressing: a good one developed during World War II is called 'Growmore'. A complete fertilizer combines the three foods that plants are most likely to need: nitrogen (N), required particularly for leaf growth, phosphates (P_2O_5) for root growth, and potash (K) for ripening fruitfulness.

Chalky and other alkaline soils have the great disadvantage of being unsuited to rhododendrons, azaleas, and most of the heathers, which are acid-loving plants. No amount of cultivation will alter the characteristics of such soils, so if you live on chalk it is best to abandon all thoughts of these delightful plants and to concentrate on the immense range of other plants which will do really well on chalk.

Chalky soils need the same treatment as sands; their main difference, in terms of preparatory treatment, is their uncultivability when wet – even walking on wet chalky soil can produce a 'pan' (layer) too dense for roots to penetrate. Drainage is naturally very quick, but this does not mean you can do without digging in humus. Alkaline clays, incidentally, need the same digging, followed by composting or gritting, as ordinary clay soils.

Above The sun rose *Cistus × purpureus*, which flowers for many weeks in summer, does well on chalk and is wind-tolerant.

Above right *Rhododendron* 'Blue Diamond' is a compact bush that flowers freely in April.

Peaty soils are easily worked and are ideal for azaleas, rhododendrons, and other members of the heath family. You may have to provide some sort of drainage system, however, as some peaty soils are impeded by an iron 'pan' of subsoil.

There are many soils that do not fall neatly into these categories: clay loam, sandy loam, peaty loam, and so on are hybrids which take their characteristics from their main constituents. Their management involves an appropriate adaptation of the main soil-type recommendations.

When working with these varying soil types it is as well to remember that nature has evolved plants to suit every conceivable variant. Seek out those which like your particular soil, and you will have found a key to happy gardening.

Planting

There are two main planting seasons: in autumn before the soil temperature falls, and in the spring; the latter is better for evergreens, when the best of their root growth lies ahead. Both seasons have their disadvantages, and a very cold, wet winter or a dry spring could make either season unsatisfactory for planting. Taking the average, how-ever, and with commonsense as our guide, it will generally be best to plant deciduous shrubs in October/November and evergreens in April, although deciduous plants can, if necessary, be planted up until mid-March. Do not plant in frozen soil.

You ought to place your order with the nurseryman in August to be sure of an early delivery. Otherwise you can, of course, visit a good garden centre to buy plants in containers; they may be a little more expensive, but at least you can choose the individual plants you fancy.

When your bundle of plants comes from the nurseryman, unpack it im-mediately. The roots will probably have no soil on them; an hour in a bucket of water or even in the garden pond will help to plump up dry roots. Next, examine the plants and remove with secateurs any pieces of root or shoot that have been broken in transit. Try to balance the size of the roots with that of the shoots above ground. Do not hesitate to cut back the shoots: it takes courage, but you will find that it pays. If you can plant straightaway, do so; otherwise dig a trench capable of holding all the roots and line the plants out thickly, covering their roots, until you are ready to plant them. This is known as 'heeling in'.

The moment of planting is the most critical in the transfer of the shrub from the nursery to your garden. Lifting at the nursery will have removed most of the tiny feeding roots or root hairs at the extreme tip of the plant's smallest roots. As only these can absorb the water which is the plant's life stream, your arrangements must ensure their speedy regrowth. For this, the fine roots need warmth and moist contact with fine soil.

The method, although simple, is very often skimped, as it takes quite a bit of patience to take out a hole *bigger* than the natural root spread. But if you do this every small root will have a chance of securing a supply of food. When planting I like to have a companion to help me and a barrow of 'planting mixture', such as peat, coarse grit, and a little bone meal. Once the plant has been comfortably set in the hole with its roots evenly spread (any long 'rogue' roots can be shortened), whoever is holding the plant must keep it upright and at the correct soil level (the level it had in the nursery, as indicated by a 'tide-mark' on the stem) while he with the shovel adds the planting mixture or fine soil. The plant should be gently joggled up and down during this process, so that the soil filters through the roots.

When the hole is half full, the soil should be firmed by treading. The rest of the hole is then filled and firmed again with the heel. Many plants are killed because they are not firmed properly, allowing them to be rocked by the wind.

Finally, finish off the job neatly; a shallow dish is the preferred shape for the soil around the base of your plant. This allows the collection of rain and dew where it is needed. Never make a mound around the stem. Use up any surplus soil by spreading it evenly over the border instead.

An exception to this rule applies to planting in really heavy, wet clay where any hole you dig tends to form a sump in which the roots will slowly drown. In this situation take a tip from some experienced planters and plant *on the surface*. Cultivate the site, adding organic matter; put in a stake half the height of the plant; place the plant in

Shrub border weeds can be dealt with in the spring by smothering with mulch of compost (as here) or other suitable material.

position and cover it with planting mixture; firm this, and finally top it off with local soil. The plant is thus on a little mound, from which it will eventually root into the soil beneath. Do not let the mound dry out for a year or two: water it if there is a drought.

The remarks above apply to shrubs in general but evergreen shrubs require additional treatment. The reason for this is that, because they have working leaves at all seasons of the year, they lose moisture at all times. Before planting an evergreen you must reduce the quantity of foliage to match that of the roots. You may feel reluctant to cut away good shoots, but doing this will double the rate of recovery (dried out shoots will turn brown and die anyway).

Regular spraying in the weeks after planting will also help to make good the loss of moisture. Evergreens should not be planted until April, when new root hairs develop rapidly. Unfortunately, the planting of evergreens needs to take place in a month when everything else in the garden seems to demand attention. You can save quite a bit of time if, during the winter, you dig out large holes where your evergreens are to go. Then mix moist, shredded peat and a complete fertilizer with the excavated soil, and fill the holes with the mixture. The April planting will then be a quick and simple job. Do not forget to put in canes to locate the holes: come the spring, you may have forgotten where you dug them!

Planting Distances

It is easy enough to say that shrubs should be planted as far apart as their anticipated width in, say, 10 years. This would mean that the largest, back-of-the-border types would be 2.5 to 3 m (8 to 10 ft) apart with the distances of the others decreasing to a minimum of about 600 mm (2 ft) for the small plants, such as cotton lavender, at the front of the border. In practice such a

Planting: first remove any pieces of root that may be damaged.

Dig a hole that is deep and wide enough not to crowd the shrub roots.

Hold the plant upright and fill the hole with a suitable planting mixture.

Firm the soil by treading with the heel. The surface should be slightly dished.

border would look so thin and unappealing that few would put up with it. You are left with two alternatives: to plant more closely (and expensively) and thin before the shrubs touch; or to put in between the permanent specimens some short-lived shrubs such as cytisus or genista until the border becomes too crowded.

After-care

There is no good reason to make the care of shrubs in any way complicated. They hate root disturbance, so the less forking you do among them the better. However, the problem of weeds will always be with us. For the first couple of seasons it is perhaps best to deal with these by hoeing, on the assumption that the weeds are all annuals, as they will be if you prepared the soil correctly. If you have not done the preparation work properly, you may have to continue to remove pieces of couch grass, ground elder, bindweed, dandelion or dock by hand, disturbing the shrubs' roots as little as possible. Once the shrubs are properly settled and growing well, you can deal with weeds either by a simazine-based weedkiller (*see* Chapter 14) or, better, by smothering them with a layer of mulch.

It is not always easy to obtain good mulch. Suitable materials include old tree leaves (usually free from your local council), bracken if you live in the right part of the country, and (best of all) farmyard or stable manure. A look at the 'Farm and Garden' advertisements in your local paper often yields surprising results: you may find, for, instance, that there is a mushroom farm near you eager to get rid of spent compost. However, the odds are you will be relying on garden compost you have made yourself. Apply about 100 g (4 oz) 'Growmore' complete fertilizer per square metre (yard) in about February; add mulch later during a mild spell, and when the earth is moist.

Compost

Some 30 years' experience of compost making have convinced me that the simplest possible method has much to commend it. I have not found that the results of others using more elaborate methods are any better, and I think anyway that the easier the routine jobs are made the more likely they are to be carried out.

In woodland compost is produced by the decomposition of fallen leaves beneath the trees. The resulting leaf mould ultimately dissolves in rainwater and feeds the plant from which it fell. The rotting process is the work of various species of bacteria, Nature's sanitary workers. The aim of your compost heap is to give these bacteria the best possible chance to rot down vegetation quickly. Here is how to go about making compost:

(1) First, always sort your decaying vegetation. Put rose prunings, hedge clippings, and any other hard and slow-rotting materials in a separate pile. When they are dry a small fire soon gets rid of them and yields wood ash, which contains very soluble potash; place the ash on the soil where it will do good right away, or store it in a dry place. Anything diseased – for example club-rooted vegetables and black-spotted rose leaves – should be burned. Of the rest, almost any plant or animal waste is useful: weeds, lawn mowings, leaves, dead flowers, potato peelings, tea leaves (*not* tea bags), tomato shoots, and herbaceous trimmings can all be used. The rotting process works better if you break up larger items of vegetation – dahlia stalks, for instance – into smaller pieces.

(2) Select a site in a corner where your compost heap will not be an eyesore. It should be about 1.2 × 2 m (4 × 6 ft) in area.

(3) Cover the base of the site with about 300 mm (1 ft) of chopped garden refuse. Tread and water well. Sprinkle on sulphate of ammonia at a rate of about 45 g/m² (1½ oz/sq yd); the nitrogen in this chemical assists bacterial action.

(4) Build up the heap in 300 mm (1 ft) layers until it is 1.2 m (4 ft) high. If you need more compost start another heap.

(5) You can speed up the action by turning the heap and adding water if it is dry; the outsides should be turned into the centre. A heap started in spring should be ready for use in the autumn; one started in the summer is likely to take until the spring.

3 Evergreen Shrubs

THE term 'evergreen' more or less explains itself: it refers to a type of plant that is always in leaf. That is not to say that such plants never lose leaves – as anyone who has done a bit of bare-handed weeding around a holly tree knows full well. But the leaves are longer-lasting than those of deciduous plants and, moreover, are shed piece-meal throughout the year rather than all at once in autumn or early winter; and, as each leaf falls, others are growing to take its place.

Take a walk in our woodlands and you are likely to see examples of one or more of four important evergreens native to Britain: holly, ivy, box, and yew. Some of the specimens you will see were probably planted a century or so ago to provide cover for game birds; in alder woods the holly and yew, in particular, may be descendants of trees that colonized the area hundreds of years ago. In more open country, our principal native evergreens are juniper, gorse, and heather.

The foliage of evergreen plants differs greatly according to the climates of the regions in which the plants originated. Evergreens such as rhododendrons and camellias, which come from humid subtropical regions with mild winters, are broad-leaved plants. In contrast, the evergreens of the colder temperate regions have much smaller leaves, which offers them greater protection against the harsher climatic conditions. Extreme examples of this type are the conifers, such as pines and firs, which have needle-like leaves. (The larch also bears needles but is deciduous.)

We in Britain are fortunate in having a climate in which extremes of heat or cold are rare and which provides abundant moisture both in the atmosphere and in the soil. Our equable climate offers a suitable environment for an enormous range of evergreens. Ever since the early 19th century British plant hunters have been bringing to these islands an immense number of evergreen shrubs from China, Japan, Burma, the Himalayas, and North and South America; and a very high proportion of these shrubs have found our climate much to their liking.

The exotic (that is, non-native) origins of many of the shrubs most popular in Britain tell us quite a lot about how best to cultivate them. For instance, the larger-leaved evergreens, which come from warmer climes than ours, are ill-adapted to survive in cold, windy sites in the garden. They are likely to flower freely only in sunny sheltered corners. Most of them are much less demanding in their pruning needs than the deciduous shrubs. They can usually be left to reach maturity with no more attention than an annual removal of any shoots which seem likely to detract from the natural shape. Some evergreens are liable to be scorched by cold winds in spring, especially if the soil is dry. 'Spring scorch' is due to sunshine and bright light. These cause leaf-growing activity and this, in turn, leads to water loss. The trouble is that the roots are not active in the cold, dry conditions and so cannot replace the lost water. As a result the leaves turn brown, and in bad cases the shrub may die. Soaking the earth and spraying the plants with water will help but badly affected branches may have to be removed.

Evergreens are slow to start into growth, many beginning only in early June. You should prune them to remove an awkward branch or evidence of spring scorch as soon as you see signs of new growth. By then the danger of fresh damage is negligible; damaged shoots can be cut out cleanly and new growths will soon restore a good shape. Do not prune in late summer or early autumn, as this would encourage young growths which might not be able to withstand the first winter frosts.

'Dead-heading' (removing old flowerheads as soon as the petals drop) can be regarded as a form of pruning. A boring job, it greatly improves plants such as azaleas and rhododendrons by preventing them from setting seed. Seed-bearing makes a great strain on a shrub's vitality, diverting resources from continued flowering.

Evergreens can broadly be grouped into those grown primarily for their flowers and those prized mainly for the beauty and form of their foliage.

The many attractive barberries include both evergreen and deciduous species. Here *Berberis darwinii*, discovered by Charles Darwin in 1835, displays a few of its clusters of attractively coloured fruits.

Flowering evergreens

The azaleas and rhododendrons are outstanding in this group, but are dealt with elsewhere (*see* Chapter 12). There are, however, many other flowering evergreens, among them some of the most beautiful of all shrubs.

Arbutus

One relative of the strawberry tree mentioned in Chapter 1 is a worthy recipient of the Award of Garden Merit: *Arbutus × andrachnoides*, which is a cross between the Irish or Killarney strawberry tree and the Grecian species *A. andrachne*. In spite of its male (Greek) parentage it is quite hardy and flowers freely in the autumn, bearing clusters of white, pitcher-shaped flowers that are followed much later by spherical strawberry-coloured fruits. One of its additional attractions is its remarkable cinnamon-red wood: few who have seen it in a shaft of sunlight on a winter's day can resist trying it. It is an especially good plant for those who garden on alkaline soils.

Barberries

Very few genera have more to offer the domestic garden than *Berberis*, the barberries. You can find attractive barberries of almost any size from 500 mm to 3 m (1½ to 10 ft) high. Most of them flower in the spring, generally with golden yellow blooms, followed by brilliant fruits, and occasionally with glowing autumn tints as well. It must be admitted that the most spectacular species are deciduous, but the evergreens are also very fine and are among the most planted of garden shrubs. One of these, *B. darwinii* was discovered by Charles Darwin in South America during his *Beagle* expedition in 1835. It starts to flower in April, bearing clusters of golden flowers which have a sheen of red-gold about their outer petals before they open. The leaves are like those of a tiny, three-pointed holly and are a shining dark green. *B. darwinii* makes a good specimen shrub some 2 m (6 ft) high.

Among its children is the even better known *Berberis × stenophylla*, one of the most graceful shrubs. Left unpruned it produces long, arching branches on which sits a multitude of rich yellow

flowers each April. It is much used as an informal hedging plant and is excellent for that purpose if there is room for it to develop freely. It was one of the first plants to receive an Award of Garden Merit, in 1923. Since then five of its progeny have been similarly honoured; all these cultivars are smaller than the 2 m (6 ft) parent. 'Autumnalis' is about half that height, but its second flowering in the autumn makes it a most desirable garden plant. 'Coccinea' (which means scarlet) actually has deep red buds which open to reveal orange flowers. It is a small plant,

as also is 'Corallina', whose branches are less tightly packed. 'Corallina' has a dwarf form, 'Corallina Compacta', which is scarcely 300 mm (1 ft) high. Finally there is 'Irwinii', a smaller edition of its parent, with golden yellow flowers.

Berberis verruculosa earns its place in the garden by its beauty of leaf as well as by its attractive, singly produced flowers. It rarely exceeds 1.5 m (5 ft) in height and forms a dense mound of glossy, dark green leaves with a white underside.

Camellias

The tremendously popular camellias usually find their way into non-alkaline gardens as named clones (individual plants derived from one original seedling or stock) or cultivars (cultivated varieties). There are no fewer than 15 with the Award of Garden Merit: I am appending the list with some hesitation because there are many hundreds of other cultivars available and the number is constantly being added to. The Award of Garden Merit is not given to plants such as the chrysanthemum and dahlia, which are continually

Camellia × williamsii 'Donation', one of the most beautiful evergreen shrubs.

being improved; but this criterion is not applied to shrubs like the camellia presumably because good cultivars remain good for very many years.

15 AGM camellias are:

Camellia 'Cornish Snow' (a hybrid; white, single flowered)
C. japonica 'Adolphe Audusson' (blood red, semi-double)
C. japonica 'Alba Simplex' (white, single)

C. japonica 'Apollo' (rose, semi-double)

C. japonica 'Contessa Lavinia Maggi' (white-overlaid rose, double)

C. japonica 'Coquetti' (rose, double)

C. japonica 'Donckelarii' (marbled red and white, double)

C. japonica 'Elegans' (rose pink, double)

C. japonica 'Gloire de Nantes' (rose pink, semi-double)

C. japonica 'Lady Clare' (peach pink, semi-double)

C. japonica 'Nagasaki' (rose-marbled white, semi-double)

C. japonica 'Preston Rose' (salmon-rose, paeony-flowered)

C. japonica 'Rubescens Major' (crimson, double)

C. 'J.C. Williams' (blush pink, single)

C. × williamsii 'Donation' (silver-pink, semi-double)

All these are excellent in their own way; but have a look also at the many other splendid camellia cultivars available. Above all, make a point of selecting from plants actually in flower.

Cultivation is very simple. Camellias need a lime-free soil and plenty of organic matter dug in where they are to be planted. They should be sheltered from cold winds by planting against walls or next to other shrubs, and they will need protection from frost and sudden thaw. Stake them until they are firmly rooted. If you fulfil these requirements you should have little to worry about. Planting is best done in April. Subsequently, dead-head after flowering, and apply a mulch of leaf mould or compost about 50 mm (2 in) deep in April.

Camellias are excellent plants for growing in tubs on a terrace or patio, and will also thrive in a cold greenhouse or conservatory.

One cannot leave the camellias without saying a few more words about the marvellous hybrid raised in Cornwall by J. C. Williams and named C. × williamsii in his honour. It has been described as the most valuable camellia hybrid ever produced, and one of its children, 'Donation', is widely regarded as the most beautiful of all evergreen shrubs. 'Donation' is erect in habit and bears semi-double flowers, rather like a double herbaceous paeony, orchid pink in colour and 100 mm

(4 in) across. Flowering may begin in mid-winter and continue until April. The flowers appear on quite young plants and, unlike all other camellias, are shed as they fade, thus making dead-heading unnecessary.

Ceanothus

The genus *Ceanothus* is a large group of plants varying in size and form from the prostrate *C. gloriosus* to the 3 m (10 ft) *C. thyrsiflorus*. The majority, however, are medium-sized shrubs which fit well into the ordinary garden and supply that rare shrub colour,

age but remain glossy. Towards the end of April and throughout May numerous tiny rich-blue flowers appear.

C. impressus is quite distinct, bearing small, deep green leaves, glossy above and downy beneath, with deep-set veins from which its species name derives. It flowers in April and May with clusters of deep-blue flowers borne with great freedom, but it needs the protection of a wall to flourish.

The remaining Award of Garden Merit ceanothus is *C. × lobbianus* which, although excellent and flowering a few weeks later than those previously men-

blue, to the scene. With their Californian origin it is not surprising that the hardiness of some is suspect. Most are happiest against a warm wall and will make a truly magnificent blue cloud when in full bloom.

One of the very best is *C.* 'Delight', worthy indeed of its name. It is one of the hardiest ceanothus, but in cold, exposed gardens it should have a sheltered spot. In southern gardens it may make a bush 3 to 4 m (10 to 13 ft) high. The leaves, a brilliant shiny green when young, turn darker with

Camellia japonica 'Donckelarii' is a first-rate plant for the open garden.

tioned, may have less garden value than *C.* 'Autumnal Blue' which, as the name suggests, flowers much later. Its panicles are large and a soft blue in colour. It has the distinction of being perhaps the hardiest of the ceanothus hybrids. 'Autumnal Blue' is vigorous with a branching habit and worth a place in any garden, for late-flowering shrubs are not numerous and blue-flowered ones are very rare.

Mexican orange blossom, *Choisya ternata*, is tolerant as to site in most southern gardens, being happy in full sun or light shade; it grows best in light, well-drained soils. It bears its white, sweet-scented flowers in May.

Elaeagnus

This genus, like *Olearia*, is valued mainly for its usefulness rather than for great beauty. Its species are widely employed for wind-resistance and for making and repairing hedges and shelter belts. Two outstanding plants for these uses are *E.* × *ebbingei*, which is adept at clambering through a thin hedge, and *E. macrophylla*, a broad-leaved Japanese species. There is, however, one gem among the utilitarian members of the genus: *E. pungens* 'Maculata', which would grace any garden. This has handsome, dark-green, oval leaves with a golden blotch imprinted within. The golden pigment impairs the food-making properties of the leaf, so slowing the plant's annual growth and ensuring that it remains a medium-sized shrub. The overall effect of this very desirable garden shrub is most striking.

Ericas

I deal with the ericas, or heaths, in more detail in Chapter 9 and elsewhere, so here I merely list the flowering evergreen kinds that have been given the AGM.

Erica arborea 'Alpina' (tree heath: white, 2 m [6 ft]; 'briar' pipes used to be made from its roots)
E. australis (Spanish heath: rose pink, 2 m [6 ft])
E. australis 'Mr Robert' (white; hardier than type)
E. carnea (rose red, 300 mm [1 ft]; winter-flowering)
E. carnea 'King George' (rose pink)
E. carnea 'Ruby Glow' (dark red)
E. carnea 'Springwood Pink'
E. carnea 'Springwood White'
E. cinerea 'C.D. Eason' (deep pink, 300 mm [1 ft])
E. cinerea 'Eden Valley' (lilac pink, 150 mm [6 in])
E. cinerea 'Knap Hill Pink'
E. cinerea 'P.S. Patrick' (purple, 300 mm [1 ft])
E. cinerea 'Rosea' (bright pink, 300 mm [1 ft])
E. × *darleyensis* 'Arthur Johnson' (magenta, 500 mm [1½ ft])
E. × *darleyensis* 'George Rendall' (rich pink)

Choisya

The Mexican orange blossom, *Choisya ternata*, is one of the most accommodating of evergreens. Equally happy in sun or shade, it will thrive in any well-drained soil. It is hardy but welcomes the protection of a wall in northern gardens. It makes a rounded shrub some 2 m (6 ft) high and as much in diameter. Its three-part leaves are a dark glossy green and give off a pungent aromatic scent when crushed. Its main glory comes in May, when a multitude of white, sweet-scented flowers appear towards the ends of its shoots. Occasional flowers continue to appear right through the summer (they are five petalled and about 25 mm (1 in) in diameter).

Clematis

The most distinguished evergreen clematis is *C. armandii*. It is a vigorous climbing plant with a height of 6 m (20 ft) and a vast spread of up to 18 m (60 ft). The glossy dark-green leaves are three-part, leathery, and with prominent veins. The flowers appear in April and are creamy white, saucer-shaped, and 50 mm (2 in) across. Two beautiful cultivars also have the Award of Garden Merit: the pure white 'Snowdrift', whose flowers are larger than those of the species, and 'Apple Blossom', whose broad sepals are white with a flush of pink within and with a deeper shading of light rose on the reverse; 'Apple Blossom' is a very desirable plant for a large sunny wall.

E. × *darleyensis* 'Silberschmelze' (this means 'molten silver', a good name for the best winter white)
E. vagans 'Lyonesse' (white, 500 mm [1½ ft])
E. vagans 'Mrs D. F. Maxwell' (deep cherry pink, 500 mm [1½ ft])
E. vagans 'St Keverne' (rose pink, 500 mm [1½ ft])

Euonymus

Euonymus fortunei is a scrambling ground coverer and a self-clinging climber at its best in the form 'Coloratus', which is richly purple and pink in foliage in the winter when starved; it may become green again in the summer.

Fatsia

Once known as *Aralia sieboldii*, *Fatsia japonica* is valued for the exotic effect created by its shape and its handsome dark-green, glossy, palmate leaves; it bears white flowers in the autumn in panicles of globular flowerheads. A variegated form develops whitish patches on the leaves.

Above left The tree heath, *Erica arborea* 'Alpina', bears scented flowers. **Below** *E. carnea* 'Springwood White', a lime-tolerant cultivar.

Above *Fatsia japonica's* globular flower panicles make an exotic effect in the autumn; they are followed by large black fruits.

Garrya

A Californian species, *Garrya elliptica* well deserves a sheltered spot in the garden. It needs neither a rich soil nor abundant moisture and the best possible place for it is a sunny, rather dry bank sloping south or west, or a wall with a similar aspect. A dark background sets off its glorious catkins to advantage. These hang all winter long clothed in a suede-like grey, but at the first surge of spring they extend themselves to their full 200 mm (8 in); then the soft grey scales lift and curl to reveal the stamens in a frilly band. It is perhaps the most spectacular catkin-bearing bush of the garden. *G. elliptica* has male and female forms, of which the former is the more spectacular. There is a good male cultivar, 'James Roof', with large, light-green, leathery leaves and extra-long catkins.

Hebe

The hebes used to be known as veronicas. None are completely hardy but they resist wind well and are therefore excellent in seaside gardens. Award of Merit forms are:

> *Hebe* 'Autumn Glory' (750 mm [2½ ft]); violet spikes from July onward)
> *H.* 'Carl Teschner' (300 mm [1 ft]); violet-blue spikes)
> *H. pinguifolia* 'Pagei' (150 to 200 mm [6 to 8 in]); white, makes a glaucous mat

Holly

The hollies (*Ilex*) are among the most accommodating of garden shrubs: they are excellent for hedges or screens or when grown as individual specimens, outstanding for their berries, spectacular in variegation, and tolerant of poor soil, smoky atmospheres, or seaside gales. AGM forms include:

> *Ilex × altaclarensis* 'Camelliifolia' (spineless leaves and big fruits)
> *I. × altaclarensis* 'Golden King' (spineless leaves with bright yellow margins; female).
> *I. × altaclarensis* 'Hodgkinsii' (very vigorous; male).
> *I. × altaclarensis* 'Wilsonii' (dense and compact; female).
> *I. aquifolium* 'Argenteomarginata'

The tassel bush, *Garrya elliptica*, shows off its spectacular silvery grey catkins to finest advantage in the spring.

(the silver holly; broad-leaved).

I. aquifolium 'Golden Queen' (a striking golden male)

Male and female parts are usually on different trees, the berries being, of course, borne only on the female plants.

Ivy

The Persian ivy, *Hedera colchica* 'Dentata Variegata', is perhaps the most spectacular of the ivies. Its leaves are large and clear green with a marbling of darker green and a deep, creamy yellow margin. It makes a really spectacular wall plant.

Kalmia

The mountain laurel or calico bush, *Kalmia latifolia*, has a fair claim to be the most beautiful of all shrubs, owing mainly to the sculptured perfection of each bud and flower in the clusters of 50 or more which make up the terminal inflorescence. Even before the flowers open each bud has a fluted precision; it opens to a shallow bowl, each segment of which is embedded and emblazoned with a deep brown anther; the whole structure is a warm and friendly pink with deeper purple markings. The leaves, too, add to the beauty of this shrub, for they have a rich glossy texture and a lively reflection.

The mountain laurel flowers in May and June following hard on the heels of the best of the rhododendron and azalea season; if it flowered a month later its marvellous qualities would be less masked by the glories of the former plants and it would no doubt be more widely planted. It will succeed well in a lightly shaded border, where it is perfectly hardy. 'Clementine Churchill' is a lovely red-flowered clone.

Osmanthus

Osmanthus delavayi was one of the first plants to receive the Award of Garden Merit, and during the 50 or so years which have elapsed since then it has proved itself one of the finest of the white-flowered evergreens. Each April the whole bush, 2 m (6 ft) or more in height, may be submerged beneath a wealth of scented tubular blossoms.

Right above The lovely flowers of *Kalmia latifolia*. **Right below** *Osmanthus delavayi* is covered in fragrant blossoms in spring.

P. mucronata needs a light peaty soil and likes full sunshine. The best known cultivar group, 'Davis's Hybrids', is about a century old and probably derives from a selection of the originals, which were raised in Northern Ireland. A very good hermaphrodite clone, 'Bell's Seedling', has large, dark red berries which, like those of the others, may last all the winter.

Pieris

All the pieris are handsome shrubs of compact habit which require the lime-free soil and growing conditions of the rhododendrons. They are valued partly for their clusters of pitcher-shaped flowers and partly for their most attractive young foliage, which may be salmon pink, red, or creamy white.

Two recommended forms are:

Pieris formosa 'Forrestii' (brilliant red young growths contrasting with glistening white flowers)

P. japonica (coppery red young foliage, large, waxy white flowers).

Pyracanthas

The firethorns are among the most popular of wall shrubs for north and east walls, but it would be a pity to confine them to that role, for they make excellent specimen shrubs. AGM forms include:

Pyracantha atalantoides (June flowers white; fruits scarlet)

P. atalantoides 'Flava', now 'Aurea' (fruits yellow)

P. coccinea 'Lalandii' (strong grower; fruits orange-red)

Above *Pyracantha atalantoides* is one of the most attractive of the autumn-fruiting firethorns. **Right** The grey foliage of *Senecio* 'Sunshine' provides an excellent foil for darker-leaved shrubs.

Pernettya

Although it is regarded basically as a ground-cover shrub (*see* Chapter 9), *Pernettya mucronata* is much more than that; standing 600 mm (2 ft) high, it makes a finer show when in fruit than most other dwarf evergreens. Its multitude of small white flowers appear in May, to be followed by marble-like berries up to 10 mm ($\frac{3}{8}$ in) in diameter in a range of colours including purple, crimson, red, pink, lilac, and white; but these will develop only if planted in groups of half a dozen female plants to one male pollinator. Good nurserymen will always provide a proven male form when you buy a batch.

P. rogersiana 'Flava' (fruits bright yellow)

P. 'Watereri' (best specimen cultivar: smothered in white flowers in June; abundant red fruits)

Generally, pyracanthas make specimens 3 m (10 ft) tall. All are hardy: given good soil, they take normally unfavourable conditions of exposure or air pollution in their stride. They all flower about the same time and are reminiscent of May blossom; the main glory is in their autumn fruits.

Senecio 'Sunshine'

You are most likely to find this excellent plant offered in catalogues under the name *Senecio laxifolius* or *S. greyii* (it received its Award of Garden Merit in 1936 as *S. laxifolius*). It is now believed that most of the plants distributed by nurserymen for many years have been hybrids of these two species and possibly of *S. complexus*. At all events, the name *S.* 'Sunshine' has the imprimatur of the Royal Botanic Gardens at Kew. It is a first-class grey-leaved plant. Not only is it one of the most pleasant grey shrubs available, but if planted near dark-foliage shrubs it enhances the latter and also serves to prevent clashes of colour among flowering plants.

The greyness of *S.* 'Sunshine' is due to a covering of silvery hairs which give its leaves good protection against rain and wind. It is therefore one of the very best seaside shrubs. It makes a lax bush about 2 m (6 ft) wide and 1 m (3 ft) high if left unpruned. I usually cut back the rather brittle shoots to about half their length in spring; this makes a more solid bush and encourages development of flowering shoots. The flowers arrive around mid-summer in clusters of bright, clear-yellow, 40 mm (1½ in) wide daisy flowers, and in such abundance as to cover the whole bush; there may also be a lesser flowering in the autumn. It is happy in any well-drained soil, is easily propagated by cuttings, and will often soil-layer itself, so making a plant to give a friend.

Skimmias

Skimmia is one of those genera which are strangely neglected, although most of the species flower and fruit readily in both acid and alkaline soils, will tolerate atmospheric pollution, and are of a size – about 1 m (3 ft) high – which makes them eminently suitable for the domestic garden. It may be that gardeners, having bought a well-berried plant from a nursery, have been disappointed at a lack of berries in succeeding years. The problem is that male and female flowers do not appear on the same plant, so that berries will be obtained only if both sexes are planted.

Skimmia japonica 'Rubella', a male form, is perhaps the first kind to plant in order to ensure berries on other plantings. This clone is a compact, rounded bush worth its place for its pleasant pale-green, leathery leaves and for the terminal panicles of red buds which give rise to its name; the buds open to reveal star-shaped flowers. Another male form, 'Fragrans', has very highly scented flowers resembling those of lily of the valley. Two other pleasing cultivars of *S. japonica* are 'Foremanii', a broad-leaved form with very large clusters of bright red fruits, and 'Rogersii', a dwarf female form with undulating leaves and exceptionally large red fruits.

The attractive berries of *Skimmia japonica*.

Viburnums

These are among the showiest and most easily grown of shrubs. All the evergreen species bear white flowers in flat heads. The laurustinus, *V. tinus*, is probably the most widely planted viburnum. It makes a billowing bush, up to 3 m (10 ft) high, with pleasant dark green, entire leaves, and bears its flowers, which are most attractive in their pink budded stage, throughout the winter months. 'Eve Price' is a variety with carmine buds and blush pink flowers. The type species has been grown and admired in this country since the 16th century.

In contrast, *V. davidii* is a dwarf plant which forms a low, wide-spreading mound. It has attractive ovate, prominently veined, glossy dark-green leaves with a paler underside. Its flowers are not specially attractive, but if male and female forms are planted together the latter may bear berries of a wonderful turquoise blue, which make a highly desirable winter feature.

Coniferous evergreens

Almost all conifers, of course, are evergreens. But only a few are worth considering in this book because the majority are quite large trees that are unsuitable for the average garden. There are, in fact, two ways in which we can approach the problem of how to enjoy the wonderful diversity of form, colour, and leaf of this great family of plants. The first is to take advantage of the fact that many genera have a tendency to 'sport' (mutate) to dwarf or semi-dwarf forms. (Quite a few gardens are devoted entirely to these naturally small forms, many of which are very attractive.) The second way is to plant species or varieties that are especially beautiful in young growth. This approach involves the necessity of making a solemn vow to yourself to remove the plants when they grow too large and begin to crowd out your other plants. The vow may be easy to make at the time. But after seven or eight years you may find it heartbreaking to have to cut down, say, a *Picea pungens glauca*, with its vivid silver-blue leaves , because it has outgrown its allotted space in your garden.

The following are among the most attractive evergreen conifers for use in the average garden.

Chamaecyparis

The name means 'false cypress' and the forms recommended here are all cultivars of Lawson's cypress, *Chamaecyparis lawsoniana*. 'Columnaris', as its name suggests, develops into a narrow upright tree, moderate in height; the foliage is bluish grey. 'Fletcherii', one of the most widely planted varieties, forms a narrow columnar bush with feathery sprays of soft grey-green foliage. Although slow-growing, it eventually becomes too big for most gardens, attaining a height of 6 m (20 ft) or more. 'Minima Aurea' is especially attractive in a rock garden, rarely exceeding 1 m (3 ft) in height; its foliage is a rich gold. 'Pygmaea Argentea' is very similar in form and size to 'Minima Aurea' but has silver foliage.

Left Two of the many attractive cultivars of *Chamaecyparis lawsoniana*: 'Stewartii' (gold) and 'Triomf van Boskoop' (blue).

Cupressus

This is the generic name of the 'true' cypresses. Perhaps the best example for the average garden is *C. glabra* 'Pyramidalis'. It is one of the most attractive of the so-called 'blue' conifers which, in fact, bear foliage of a rich, gleaming, bluish green. 'Pyramidalis' develops into a medium-sized conical tree.

Juniperus

This genus includes some of the most useful evergreen conifers for smaller gardens; most of them have the added advantage of being much more tolerant of chalky (lime-rich) soils than other conifers. *J. horizontalis* is one of several prostrate (ground-hugging) species that make excellent cover for hot, sunny banks. *J. × media* 'Pfitzeriana' is one of the most useful of all garden conifers, making a pleasant, wide-spreading shrub suitable as a specimen, as ground cover, for clothing a difficult shady corner, or as a feature marking, say, a confluence of garden paths. An attrac- tive variant is 'Golden Pfitzer'. *J. sabina tamariscifolia* is an aptly named 1 m (3 ft) sprawler, whose spiky foliage reminds one of the tamarisk. It is suitable equally as a specimen or as ground cover.

Taxus baccata

This species, the common yew, is rather too sombre in appearance for most gardens except for hedges. But two varieties of the species have found favour with owners of smaller gardens. 'Lutea' develops attractive yellow cups to hold its single seeds which are pro- duced in abundance. 'Semperaurea', one of the slower-growing varieties, has attractive leaves that are golden yellow on opening and shade with age to golden brown. Among yews in general, male and female forms are on separate trees, so you must plant examples of both forms if you wish your varieties to produce berries. Inci- dentally, the seeds are poisonous – a point to bear in mind if you have young children. Yews must not be grown where there is any risk of cattle browsing. The foliage, especially when wilted after clipping, is toxic to them.

Thuja

This genus includes a number of slow- growing shrubs. *T. occidentalis* 'Rhein- gold' is one of the best, especially if it is planted against a dark-green back- ground, when its rich golden-yellow foliage with a hint of brown is seen at its most attractive. Of bushy habit, 'Rheingold' may outgrow a small gar- den in about 15 years. *T. orientalis* 'Aurea Nana', the Chinese equivalent of the above, is a genuinely dwarf form. It grows into a dense, rounded bush, usually with pale-green foliage which may be tipped with yellow.

Juniperus sabina 'Tamariscifolia', with its horizontal tiers of spiky branchlets, is one of the most useful of the ground-hugging conifers for the smaller garden. Like other junipers, it will flourish in chalky soils.

4 Deciduous Shrubs

THESE are the shrubs which shed their leaves in the autumn, remain bare during the winter, and burst into fresh leaf in the spring. Autumnal leaf-shedding is a device that helps plants to survive cold winters. The very fact that a plant is deciduous is an indication that it hails from a climate similar to our own and is probably quite hardy. Some of the most abundantly flowering of all shrubs are of this type. As there is an enormous number that are potentially suitable for the smaller garden, I will concentrate here on some of the most distinguished recipients of the AGM.

Abelia × grandiflora
One of the best of the late-summer-flowering shrubs, this hybrid is hardier and more vigorous than either of its parents. A good specimen may be 2 m (6 ft) high. It has graceful, arching branches bearing brilliant green foliage and, from July to September, clusters of pale pink and white bell-shaped flowers about 20 mm ($\frac{3}{4}$ in) long. It is a particularly useful shrub, as it flowers when little else does.

Aesculus parviflora
Although this North American shrub is related to the horse chestnut, it is quite unlike the latter except in the appearance of its flowerheads. It is a suckering shrub, growing to about 3 m (10 ft) high, which makes an attractive solitary specimen on a large lawn. It flowers in July and August, a most welcome time for shrubs, bearing white candelabra with deep red anthers, and

it has the added bonus of attractive foliage colour in autumn.

Buddleia
The weeping buddleia (B. alternifolia) gets its common name from its habit of producing a multitude of graceful,

arching branches that sweep down to the ground. These are set in June with tight clusters of lilac-coloured flowers, creating a graceful waterfall of pale blue. It makes a most attractive 3 m (10 ft) lawn specimen. A word of

caution, however: on alkaline (chalky) soils the shrub will grow satisfactorily, but its flowers are a less charming pinkish colour.

Buddleia davidii is one of the most widely grown of all shrubs in Britain. It became familiar to many city dwellers after World War II, when its great natural vigour enabled wind-blown seeds to colonise often indifferent soil on abandoned bomb sites. That the flowers of these wild-growing plants were not always of good colour emphasizes the importance of selecting cultivars of high quality. B. davidii bears 300 to 400 mm (12 to 16 in) flower spikes in mid-summer, when it fully earns its common name of 'butterfly bush'. Among the best cultivars are:
'Black Knight' (very deep purple flowers, which benefit from a pale background)
'Empire Blue' (a yellow eye sets off its deep blue)
'Fortune' (pale lilac with orange-yellow eye)
'Royal Red' (magnificent red-purple)
'White Profusion' (a yellow eye in a pure white flower)

Caryopteris × clandonensis
This is one of the best of the small, late-flowering, blue shrubs for the garden. If pruned well back each year it forms a blue cloud about 500 mm ($1\frac{1}{2}$ ft) high in August and September, and

Left The graceful June-flowering *Buddleia alternifolia*. Right *Ceratostigma willmottianum*, one of the best late-summer-flowering dwarf shrubs, likes a dry, well-drained soil.

with its light grey-green foliage it makes a fine mid-border plant.

Ceanothus 'Gloire de Versailles'

Most of the worthwhile ceanothus are evergreen (*see* Chapter 3). 'Gloire de Versailles' is a cultivar of a deciduous species – the best of the half dozen or so which make up its group. Like all ceanothus it enjoys full sun and good drainage. A late flowerer (July and August), it can be cut back each spring to encourage new growths that will throw up large panicles of the small, pale blue flowers. It is a good plant for the mixed border.

Ceratostigma willmottianum

This is a beautiful blue-flowered, summer- and autumn-flowering dwarf shrub. Miss Willmott, the noted gardener after whom it is named, received seeds collected in China. Only two germinated, and these have provided the stock from which all the plants in cultivation have been derived. The rich blue flowers appear in clusters at the ends of the branches, which are usually about 600 mm (2 ft) high and break freely from the base of the plant. The first flowers are seen in July and it is still flowering when the frosts come, by which time the foliage has a red autumnal tinge.

Chaenomeles speciosa and C. × superba

The ornamental quinces, or 'japonicas', are among the least demanding shrubs regarding soil and cultivation; they are also among the most beautiful when, long before a leaf is seen, their flowers – shallow bowls of scarlet, orange, pink, or white – button themselves along the branches. Later their fruits, the yellowish quinces (which make a good jelly), appear. A number of cultivars have the AGM, including 'Knap Hill Scarlet', the most brilliant of all red kinds; 'Cardinalis', rich crimson; 'Moerloosii', delicate pink to white; 'Phyllis Moore', semi-double, salmon pink; 'Simonii', dwarf, deep scarlet; and 'Scarlet and Gold', in which golden anthers are set off by scarlet petals.

Corylopsis

This genus has the great advantage of producing flowers in early spring, long before most other garden shrubs. Most

species produce tassels of fragrant, pale yellow flowers, are easy to grow, thrive in ordinary soils (preferably in sheltered positions), and need little pruning. *C. glabrescens* is probably the best species for chalky soils. *C. pauciflora* prefers acid or neutral soils. Its species name means 'few-flowered' – a reference not to its total number of flowers (which is great) but to the fact that each tassel contains only two or three blooms.

Cytisus

Commonly known as broom, this genus includes many useful cultivars and hybrids, many derived from *C. scoparius*. These grow very rapidly and have a tendency to become top-heavy; they require stout supporting stakes. Prune them after flowering, cutting back to produce a firm head of young

Cytisus × beanii, a dwarf hybrid, creates a brilliant display in May.

growth; but be careful not to cut into the hard wood, as this might kill the plant. Being short-lived, these are good plants to use as fillers between more durable kinds. Among the best are the cultivars 'Cornish Cream', 'Firefly' (orange and bronze), and 'Golden Sunlight'; and the natural variety *C. scoparius sulphureus* (cream and sulphur).

The Moroccan broom, *C. battandieri*, also grows fast and needs support. It is less hardy than *C. scoparius* and its cultivars, and will benefit from the protection of a wall. Do not use wire to support it, or it will strangle itself in a couple of years. It bears silky foliage, which seems to light up when gentle winds turn the leaves, and large, upright cones of bright yellow flowers; it has a strong, fruity scent. It needs to be cut back after flowering or it will soon outgrow a small garden.

The *Cytisus* hybrids also include a number of small shrubs, less than 1 m (3 ft) high, that make attractive additions to the rock garden or other site where a brilliant two- or three-week display of flowers will be welcome. All appreciate plenty of sun and a light soil. Among the best are *C. × beanii* (golden yellow); *C. × kewensis* (cream); *C. × praecox* (cream); and *C. × praecox* 'Allgold' (rich yellow).

Deutzia

The best of the summer-flowering deutzias are medium-sized hybrids, many of them produced by the great 19th-century French nurseryman Victor Lemoine at Nancy. Deutzias are vigorous growers, producing small but abundant flowers that are white or various shades of pink in colour. They prefer warm, sunny places and need little pruning. The following are especially good: *D. × elegantissima* (bright rose-pink flowers); *D. × hybrida* 'Magicien' (mauve-pink overlaid with purple and white); *D. × hybrida* 'Mont Rose' (abundant rose-pink flowers); *D. × magnifica* (double white); and *D. × rosea* 'Carminea' (perhaps the best of a number of excellent clones of this hybrid).

Forsythia × intermedia

This is one of the best and most popular of the early-flowering shrubs. A very vigorous grower, reaching 3 to 4.5 m (10 to 15 ft), it produces an enormous abundance of golden yellow bells each spring. It roots freely from hard-wood cuttings. Two forms of this species are especially good for gardens: the natural variety *spectabilis*, which flowers in late March or April; and the cultivar 'Lynwood', which flowers slightly later but produces larger blooms.

Fuchsia

Except in the mildest parts of these islands, fuchsias lead an herbaceous existence; that is, they die back above ground during the winter but shoot up afresh the next spring. Therefore you should not regard them as being hardy in the sense that ericas or forsythias are, and you should plant them

Fuchsia 'Mrs Popple', an old favourite, is one of the hardiest members of this genus.

in a sunny, well-drained part of the garden. In colder districts, sprinkle a shovelful of coarse grit around the crown before the first frosts of autumn. Most forms attain a height of 600 mm to 1.2 m (2 to 4 ft) and a somewhat larger spread.

I have selected my two favourites out of 10 forms that have the AGM. The natural variety *F. magellanica gracilis* develops slender, arching branches bearing smallish, pendant red and violet flowers in great abundance. The cultivar 'Mrs Popple' is similar in form, and bears flowers in which coral-red sepals enclose a bright purple corolla. Hardier than most fuchsias, 'Mrs Popple' has been grown in England for many years.

Genista

This genus is closely related to *Cytisus* and the two are often found attractively associated in heather gardens. The different species offer the gardener a wide choice in terms of size and flowering season; all grow in soil of indifferent quality but thrive best in warm, sunny locations. The following are three of the best. *G. aetnensis*, Mount Etna broom, has largely dispensed with leaves in favour of weeping green shoots that are attractive throughout the growing season. It reaches its full glory, however, in July and August, when it becomes a veritable waterfall of abundant golden flowers. The largest of my selection, it can reach a height of 3.5 m (12 ft) and more. *G. lydia*, in contrast, is rarely more than 600 mm (2 ft) high and an outstanding dwarf

shrub. It is most effective when planted on a low wall or on a high point in a rock garden; its bright yellow flowers appear on pendulous, grey-green branches in May and June. Even smaller is G. *tinctoria*, dyer's greenweed, which averages 300 to 600 mm (1 to 2 ft) in height. Its cultivar 'Royal Gold' is one of the finest late-flowering dwarf shrubs. Although it begins to flower soon after mid-summer, its stems continue to be covered in rich yellow flowers until September. A plant native to Britain, the species was once important in the dyeing industry, as its name indicates. It was used to manufacture a rich yellow dye which, when mixed with an extract of woad (this provided another vegetable dye, a blue)

produced the once-famous Kendal Green dye.

Halesia carolina

This, the silver bell or snowdrop tree, is a native of North America. As it has a spreading habit and will eventually attain a height of 6 m (20 ft) it must be regarded as a temporary resident of small gardens. Nonetheless, its bell-shaped, silvery white flowers make a charming addition to the garden in May. The tree will grow only in lime-free soils.

Hibiscus syriacus

The shrubby or tree mallow is not, in fact, native to Syria but to India and China. Not surprisingly, it needs a

The free-spreading snowdrop tree, *Halesia carolina*, makes a fine specimen for larger gardens. It requires an acid soil.

warm, sunny position and good, well-drained soil if it is to flower with the abandon of which it is capable. Given these conditions, it is quite hardy, and will attain a height of about 2.5 m (8 ft) and a width of 3 m (10 ft). It flowers from August to October, producing mallow-like blooms. Good cultivars include 'Woodbridge' (rich rosy crimson flowers with darker red central blotches); 'Hamabo' (pale blush pink with a crimson centre); 'Blue Bird' (a very good single, blue with a darker eye); and 'William R. Smith' (single, pure white).

Hydrangea

By far the best-known examples of this genus are the 'mopheads' of the greenhouse and florist's shop – the cultivars of the Hortensia group derived from *Hydrangea macrophylla*. None of these has the AGM, owing to their unreliability out of doors; but if you live in a warm area in the south or west of England, preferably near the sea, and can provide a good, sheltered site, the following members of the group can be recommended: 'Altona', a shade-loving variety with rose pink flowers; 'Joseph Banks', with very large cream to pink heads; 'Goliath', with deep pink flowers; and 'Mme E. Mouillière', with superb white flowers.

There is, however, a great deal more to this great genus than the mopheads. *H. paniculata* 'Grandiflora' must be one of the most spectacular of all the larger shrubs flowering in August and September. Fully grown it may be 4 to 5 m (13 to 16 ft) high, with each terminal growth ending in a creamy white inflorescence which turns pinkish and in mass forms a cascade. A smaller, earlier cultivar, 'Praecox', flowers in July and is perhaps better suited to small gardens than the later 'Grandiflora'.

Another group derived from *H. macrophylla* is the lacecaps, which produce their flowers in a flattened terminal head: an outer ring of infertile but very showy ray florets surrounding usually lighter-coloured and less attrac-

Hydrangea 'Blue Wave' is one of the best of the popular lacecaps. On alkaline soils this cultivar bears pink flowers.

tive female flowers. As with other hydrangeas, the colours of lacecaps depend on the type of soil in which they are growing. The beautiful blue shades are produced only on acid soils, while alkaline soils produce colours varying from white, through rosy pink, to reddish purple. Two of the most attractive lacecap cultivars are 'Bluewave' (its outer ring of false petals may be blue or pink according to the soil while the central florets are always purplish blue), and 'Veitchii' (which thrives on chalk soils and produces white blooms).

Hypericum patulum 'Hidcote', semi-evergreen.

Hypericum

The genus includes a number of deciduous and evergreen shrubs producing flowers throughout the summer. One of the best is the 'Hidcote' cultivar of *H. patulum*, which has a bushy habit and grows to about 2 m (6 ft) high and wide; its rich yellow bowl-shaped flowers are the largest of any of the hypericums. *H. calycinum*, the Rose of Sharon, a semi-evergreen like 'Hidcote', is shorter, with a more spreading habit, and makes an excellent cover for a hot, dry bank of chalky soil. Both forms are simple to grow, and are easily propagated from cuttings after the flowers have finished.

Kerria japonica

There are few medium-sized shrubs which are easier or more rewarding in March and April than the Jew's Mallow, as this plant is commonly known. It will grow unsupported to a height of about 2 m (6 ft), but it is often treated as a climber and trained up a fence or wall; it spreads freely by means of underground suckers. Its green stems in winter, bright yellow, star-shaped flowers in April and May, and attractive foliage from spring to autumn make a valuable contribution to any garden. The species bears single flowers; there is also a double form, *K. japonica* 'Pleniflora', producing bright orange-yellow blooms about 40 mm ($1\frac{1}{2}$ in) in diameter. It was introduced from China in 1700 and has been popular ever since.

Lavandula

Lavender must surely be among the best-loved of all shrubs. Grown for centuries, it has so many good qualities: a grey colour which blends and contrasts well with greens; subtle blue flowers; flowerheads which, whether on the plant or gathered and dried, provide a delightful, long-lasting aroma; tolerance of clipping to make an internal garden hedge; and a natural affinity for roses, especially pink varieties. The garden cultivars are mostly derived from *Lavandula spica*, and differ considerably in size and in shade of flower colour. 'Hidcote' is perhaps the best of many cultivars. It is a compact plant, about 600 mm (2 ft) high, with deep purple-violet flowers on dense,

50 mm (2 in) spikes. Like other varieties it likes a light, well-drained soil in a sunny position.

Philadelphus

The mock oranges are beautiful, usually white-flowered shrubs, heavily scented, and up to 4 m (13 ft) high. (Many gardeners wrongly call them 'syringa', which is the botanical name of the lilac. 'Mock orange' is, in fact, an apter name, for the large flowers of *Philadelphus* are similar to the blossom of the orange tree.) The flowers bloom in June and July, just as the main shrub season is waning. The best mock oranges for the ordinary garden are hybrids. Although many will grow to a considerable height, they can be restricted to about 1 m (3 ft) if you cut all flowering shoots right back to their origin immediately the flowers are over. This will leave a mass of young shoots, which may be thinned down to nine or ten in number. All the plant's vigour will now be concentrated into these growths, which will flower with remarkable abundance the following summer. The following hybrids all have the AGM.

P. 'Avalanche' gained its name from the arching habit of its branches, which are bowed down by the weight of the sweet-scented, single, white flowers borne in clusters of seven. *P.* 'Beauclerk', one of the few *Philadelphus* hybrids not raised by Victor Lemoine of Nancy, bears 70 mm (2½ in) flowers with pale purple centres. *P.* 'Belle Étoile' belongs to the group whose milk-white petals have a purple blotch in the centre; they are deliciously scented and very free-flowering. *P.* 'Sybille' is one of the smaller hybrids, some 1.5 m (5 ft) high; it has gracefully arching growths bearing curiously shaped, almost rectangular flowers which are white and slightly fringed, with a rosy purple stain marking the centre.

Finally, if your garden is large enough, give thought to *P. pubescens* or its close relative *P. intectus*, which gardeners have tended to ignore in favour of the hybrids. Perhaps the finest representative of the genus, it may grow to 3.5 m (12 ft) or more, and bears magnificent, pure white flowers some 50 mm (2 in) in diameter.

Mock orange *P.* × *virginalis* 'Virginal'.

Potentilla fruticosa cultivars are among the most useful and trouble-free of all garden shrubs.

Potentilla

The shrubby cinquefoils are among the most versatile flowering plants in the garden. They are dwarf shrubs which flower continuously throughout the summer, thrive in any reasonably fertile soil, are rarely troubled by pests or disease, make excellent weed smotherers, and, although sun-loving, will tolerate all but deep shade. The following varieties and hybrids are among the best of the AGM winners.

P. 'Elizabeth', one of the most useful of small shrubs, is up to 1 m (3 ft) high and is spangled with rich, soft yellow flowers 40 mm ($1\frac{1}{2}$ in) in diameter from June to October. It looks especially attractive on top of a dwarf wall. P. *fruticosa* 'Beesii', which is worth growing for its silvery foliage alone, bears attractive golden flowers. P. *fruticosa* 'Katherine Dykes' is one of the taller varieties – up to 2 m (6 ft) high – and bears canary yellow flowers; it makes a very good internal garden hedge. P. *fruticosa mandshurica* (a natural variety sometimes catalogued as a cultivar, P. *fruticosa* 'Manchu') is a groundhugger, rarely more than 300 mm (1 ft) high, and bears spangles of white flowers over a very long period.

You might also like to try some recently introduced P. *fruticosa* cultivars that bear flowers of quite different colours. Two of the more promising are 'Red Ace' and 'Tangerine'.

Rubus

This is the genus to which garden brambles and the raspberry belong. As a whole the flowering shrubs in this group tend to be too vigorous for smaller gardens, but two AGM holders are well worth considering. R. *deliciosus* is a bramble which bears no thorns and rarely exceeds 2 m (6 ft) in height and width. Its flowers, pure white cups resembling a single rose 50 mm (2 in) in diameter, are borne on short side growths from the previous year. Little pruning is necessary save of old, worn-out growths. *Rubus × tridel* 'Benenden', a delightful clone, is a more vigorous shrub, reaching 3 m (10 ft). The stems are thornless and flower with the greatest freedom, bearing pure white 50 mm (2 in) flowers set off by a central boss of yellow stamens. It propagates easily from layers or half-ripe cuttings.

Spiraea

The shrubby spiraeas are a large and important group of ornamental plants. The two I have selected offer alternatives in both size and flowering season. S. × *arguta* is perhaps the best of the spring-flowering spiraeas; it has narrow oval leaves and pretty spring-green, slender, arching stems densely set with flat, pure white clusters of flowers in late April and May. It grows to a maximum height and width of about 2.5 m (8 ft). *Spiraea × bumalda* 'Anthony Waterer' is a most valuable front-of-the-border shrub which can be kept less than 1 m (3 ft) high if pruned hard early in the spring each year. It then throws up young shoots, each crowned with a broad, flat, rich crimson panicle of flowers; the shoots are occasionally variegated with pink and cream.

Syringa

The syringas, better known by their common name, lilacs, are among the best-loved shrubs in the garden. Their wild-growing range is enormous – from Iran to China – and there are many beautiful but little-known species, while plant breeders in Europe and America have developed more than 1,000 cultivars. Our domesticated lilacs are versatile, tolerant shrubs, growing happily in the most hostile urban atmospheres and in most soils (although they prefer alkaline to acid types). It is this very tolerance that is responsible for the many lilacs of poor quality one can observe in gardens in May and June. Until quite recently it was common practice to graft a cultivar on to a wild lilac stock. The resulting plant suckers readily, and if the suckers (recognizable by their lighter colour) are not removed at once they will take over the plant – leaving a wild lilac instead of a cultivar. Many such wild plants are attractive in their own way, but cannot compare in form or colour with the best cultivars, and moreover they are much too large for the average garden. The following list of reliable species, hybrids, and cultivars is large enough to enable you to make an attractive selection.

Syringa × chinensis Known as the Rouen lilac (it was raised in that city's Botanic Garden some 200 years ago), this is a dense, bushy, medium-sized shrub with ovate leaves and fragrant, soft purple flowers which appear in May. Three clones of the species have the AGM: 'Alba' (white flowers), 'Metensis' (pale pink), and 'Saugiana' (deep pink).

Syringa microphylla 'Superba'. This cultivar is a stronger, taller plant than the parent species. It has privet-like leaves and rosy lilac flowers in May, and is distinguished from all other

Right *Spiraea × bumalda* 'Anthony Waterer'.

lilacs by continuing to flower inter-mittently until October.

Syringa × josiflexa 'Bellicent'. This is one of the best of many superb hybrid cultivars raised by Isabella Preston. When full-grown it may be as much as 4 m (13 ft) high and wide, with broad, deep green, ovate leaves. The flowers come in early June – great panicles of fragrant, clear, rose-coloured blooms.

Syringa velutina. The lovely Korean lilac rarely exceeds 2 m (6 ft) in height. In May its small-leaved foliage vir-tually disappears in a cloud of pale pink, very fragrant flowers. It has been wrongly described as a dwarf lilac. You can, in fact, restrict its rate of growth if you plant it where its roots are confined.

Syringa vulgaris. The common lilac needs no recommendation from me: it has been beloved in its hundreds of cultivar forms for more than a hundred years, and many of the best date from the 19th century. The 11 mentioned below cannot begin to do justice to the total number available, but they are at least representative of the most popular colours in single and double flower forms available. In general the singles are considered to be the more graceful, while the doubles tend to display lon-ger. Note that the colour refers to that of the half-opened flowers: there is variation in the colours of the opening buds and the fading flowers.

Colour	Single	Double
White	'Maud Notcutt'	'Mme Lemoine'
Lilac/Blue	'Firmament'	'Michael Buchner'
Pink/ Mauve	'Paul Thirion'	'Katharine Havemeyer' 'Mme Antoine Buchner'
Magenta	'Massena'	'Mrs Edward Harding'
Purple	'Souvenir de Louis Spaeth'	'Charles Joly'

Left above May-flowering *Syringa × chinensis* 'Alba', one of the Rouen lilacs. **Left below** June-flowering *Syringa × josiflexa*, a Canadian hybrid. The hardy syringas, with their upright or arching flowers, can be used as a lawn feature, in the border, or even as hedging plants.

Tamarix

The tamarisk is found, in wild-growing form, from southern Europe eastwards to China. (A resinous sap, exuded by the plants when they are attacked by a scale insect, is believed to have been the 'manna' that fed the ancient Israelites in the desert.) Most of the tamarisk species are very hardy plants that thrive in dryish soil in full sun. They are easy to grow, requiring little more attention than the removal of old, spent wood after the flowering season. To propagate them, all that is necessary is to take pieces about the size of a light walking stick or smaller and push them to half their length into cultivated soil in the autumn; they will have rooted by the spring. Two species have the AGM. The May-flowering *Tamarix parviflora* will probably be familiar to you if you take your holidays by the Mediterranean. It bears its pale pink flowers on slender, arching branches that are a deep, vinous purple in colour. Perhaps even finer is *T. pentandra*. Its tiny flowers are arranged in long, branching racemes which in August transform the shoots into rosy plumes up to 1 m (3 ft) in length. *T. pentandra* is a much more vigorous grower than *T. parviflora,* and can attain a height and width of 4.5 m (15 ft) if left unchecked. If you have a small garden, cut the plant back hard in February to encourage strong new growths.

Weigela

The weigelas, sometimes known as bush honeysuckles, are decorative and very easily grown shrubs of up to 2.5 m (8 ft) height and spread. Most like good, moist soil and plenty of sun. The plants bear bell-shaped flowers in May and June, after which you should cut back the flower-bearing shoots. Propagate by half-ripe cuttings in July or by hard wood cuttings in October. Two good hybrids are *Weigela* 'Abel Carrière', with yellow-throated red-carmine flowers, and *W.* 'Bristol Ruby', a more erect plant bearing ruby red flowers.

Tamarix pentandra, probably the best of the late-flowering tamarisks, thrives on exposed sites, preferably in lime-free soils. For small gardens this vigorous grower can be kept to a moderate height and spread if it is cut back hard in February.

5 Special Effects

WHEN planning your shrub garden you will probably begin with a selection of your personal favourites and then, perhaps, add to the list some varieties you have admired in private or public gardens. This makes a good start, but the final effect of a garden depends not only on the beauty of individual plants but also on the way the design exploits interesting blends and contrasts of colour and form. No doubt you will have your own ideas about this, but the following notes may help beginners.

Variegation

This is a term used to describe foliage of which the normal colour, usually green, is patterned or spotted with contrasting hues, usually white, cream, or grey but sometimes other colours. In some individual plants variegation is caused by disease, but in the cultivars and varieties we are concerned with it is inherent. Such leaves contain less chlorophyll, a pigment that gives leaves their characteristic green colour. Chlorophyll is the substance that triggers a leaf's food-making activities, so that plants with variegated foliage are generally less vigorous than non-variegated forms of the same species and are more easily killed by drought or extremes of cold. Many variegated shrubs have a tendency to produce wholly green shoots now and again. These must be pruned out as soon as possible or they will take over the plant.

The garden would certainly be a poorer place without the contrasts provided by variegated shrubs but I would like to sound a warning against their over-use: too many variegated plants unalleviated by normal forms can produce a spotty effect, giving rise to a visually disturbing atmosphere.

Following are a few of the shrubs with specially attractive variegation.

Acer negundo
One of the smaller members of the maple family, this tree can nevertheless reach a height of 7.5 m (25 ft). However, it readily accepts being cut back to fit the smaller garden. The attractive, typically maple leaves are set off by yellow variegation in the cultivar 'Elegans' and by silver in 'Variegatum'.

Cornus
The dogwoods include two useful variegated cultivars. *C. alba* 'Spaethii' (golden yellow) is considered by many to have the handsomest variegation of any deciduous shrub. It should be planted in small groups, and the quality of variegation is best maintained by cutting back hard in the spring. *C. controversa* 'Variegata' is unusual both for its silvery variegation and for its distinctively horizontal branching. It also provides a bonus of creamy white flower clusters in June and July and black berries in the autumn. Both these cultivars grow about 3 m (10 ft) tall, 'Variegata' being the slower growing.

Elaeagnus
E. pungens 'Maculata', a dense and handsome bush which can attain a height and width of 3 m (10 ft) or more but is slow growing, is one of several cultivars of this evergreen that are noted for their variegation all the year round. In 'Maculata' the shiny green leaves are splashed with gold.

Euonymus
These shrubs are so tolerant that they rarely receive the care and attention they need to make their best showing. One of the best is *E. fortunei* 'Silver Queen', a shrub of creeping habit that will reach a height of 3 m (10 ft) if planted against a warm wall. For most of the year the deep green leaves are

Left *Acer negundo* 'Variegatum', an elegant small maple. **Right** *Prunus* 'Kiku-shidare Sakura', an attractive pendular, spring-flowering Japanese cherry.

edged in creamy white, but in early spring the young leaves open a creamy yellow colour with a paler border. *E. japonicus* 'Ovatus Aureus', a cultivar of a popular hedging shrub for coastal gardens, has very attractive golden yellow variegation.

Hebe

H. × franciscana 'Variegata' is slightly less hardy than the hybrid type, but it will flourish in a sheltered corner, producing its creamy variegated leaves all the year round.

Ilex

There are two excellent clones of *I. aquifolium*, the broad-leaved common holly: 'Argenteomarginata' (silver variegation) and 'Golden Queen' (deep yellow).

Pittosporum

This genus contains some of the most beautiful of all the evergreen shrubs. Unfortunately, most of them are too tender to thrive outdoors in this country. Hardier than most is *P. tenuifolium*, a native of New Zealand, which is well worth trying if you live in a warmer part of the south or west. Two cultivars with variegation are 'Silver Queen' (silvery white) and 'Variegatum' (creamy white). In both, the colours contrast strikingly with the black stems.

Rhamnus alaterna

Related to our native alder buckthorn, *R. frangula*, this shrub is a native of the Mediterranean region and needs a warm, sunny spot, preferably near the sea. The cultivar 'Argenteovariegata' bears striking marbled grey leaves with cream variegation.

Weigela florida

This is a very popular medium-sized shrub bearing pink, bell-shaped flowers in May and June. The cultivar 'Variegata' has cream-edged leaves.

Right above *Hebe × franciscana* 'Variegata' (backed here by *Smilacina racemosa* in autumn colour) produces its distinctively variegated foliage throughout the year.
Right below The golden elder, *Sambucus nigra* 'Aurea', produces consistently golden leaves, especially in poor soils, and will thrive in shady corners. The tree attains a height of about 3 m (10 ft) and benefits from hard spring pruning.

Unusual leaf colours

The following are some foliage shrubs which make their effect not by the variegation of their leaves but because the leaves are of a single striking colour other than green. Many popular shrubs include a form which displays this feature.

Cotinus coggyria 'Royal Purple' is one of the finest purple-foliage shrubs.

Silver

Artemisia arborescens (lad's love)
Calluna 'Silver Grey'
Convolvulus cneorum (a dwarf)
Cytisus battandieri (Moroccan broom)
Halimium atriplicifolium
Potentilla fruticosa 'Beesii'
Santolina chamaecyparissus (cotton lavender)
Senecio 'Sunshine'

Gold

If you are looking through the catalogues, cultivars called 'Aurea' or 'Aureum' are a reliable indication that their foliage is gold (from Latin *aureus*, golden).

Acer japonicum 'Aureum' (golden Japanese maple)
Calluna 'Gold Feather'
Calluna 'Gold Haze'
Calluna 'Joy Vanstone'
Cornus alba 'Aurea' (golden dogwood)
Erica carnea 'Aurea'
Erica cinerea 'Gold Haze'
Ligustrum ovalifolium 'Aureum' (golden privet)
Philadelphus coronarius 'Aureus' (golden mock orange)
Sambucus nigra 'Aurea' (golden elder)
Sambucus racemosa 'Plumosa Aurea'
Syringa emodi 'Aurea'

Purple

'Purpurea' or 'Purpureum' in a cultivar's name indicates purple foliage (from *purpure*, Old English for heraldic purple).

Acer palmatum 'Dissectum atropurpureum'
Berberis × ottawensis 'Purpurea'
Berberis vulgaris 'Atropurpurea'
Corylus maxima 'Purpurea'
Cotinus coggyria 'Royal Purple'
Prunus spinosa 'Purpurea'

Rich brown

Stephanandra tanakae (a Japanese shrub related to the spiraeas)
Hydrangea bretschneideri
Both of these maintain their bark colour without pruning

Purple

Salix daphnoides (violet willow; its colour is overlaid by a waxy bloom)
Salix acutifolia (deeper purple shoots with a white bloom). Both these need hard spring pruning

Green

Kerria japonica (slender, twiggy, bright green shoots)
Leycesteria formosa (hollow, blue-green shoots with a slight bloom)

Colour changes

We all delight in the turn of green leaves of deciduous trees to glorious browns and golds in the autumn. One of the most interesting recent developments has been the introduction of evergreen shrub cultivars whose leaves change colour from season to season. The most striking of these are clones of *Calluna vulgaris*, the common heather of the English and Scottish countryside. Among the finest of these clones are 'Blazeaway', which is green in summer and rich red in winter; 'Golden Feather', light gold in summer, deeper gold in winter; 'Gold Haze', a 600 mm (2 ft) heather with bright yellow leaves; and 'Robert Chapman', pale gold in spring, orange in summer, and red in winter.

Unusual forms

Occasionally, an individual plant will assume a form quite different from others of its species. Such aberrant forms can sometimes be perpetuated by plant propagators, resulting in cultivars of unusual and sometimes attractive shapes. Two such aberrations are a very upright form (called 'fastigiate'), and a drooping ('pendulous') form, as in the weeping willow. Neither form is very common among shrubs, but each includes several hybrids or cultivars that could make attractive additions to the garden.

Fastigiates
Cultivars of this form are usually called 'Stricta' (or 'Strictus') or 'Erecta' (or 'Erectus'). At present there are about half a dozen deciduous genera.
BERBERIS THUNBERGII is one of the most attractive deciduous shrubs, producing abundant red berries and brilliant orange and scarlet foliage in the autumn. The fastigiate form, 'Erecta', is ideal as a hedging shrub of 1 to 1.5 m (3 to 5 ft); it is more or less dog-proof, and needs little maintenance apart from occasional removal of unshapely shoots.

Left above *Calluna* 'Robert Chapman' and 'Silver Queen'. **Left below** *Philadelphus* 'Erectus'.

ULEX EUROPAEUS is another excellent hedging plant in its 'Strictus' form, developing abundant spines, although it bears fewer flowers than most other gorses.

Other deciduous fastigiates include *Crataegus monogyna* 'Stricta'. a hawthorn, *Philadelphus erectus*, and *Erica terminalis*, the Corsican heath.

There are abundant coniferous fastigiates. Most, however, develop into large trees and so are useful in the shrub garden for only about 6 to 12 years. Probably the best way to use these conifers is as solitary lawn specimens or as a pair to define a vista or to make a contrast with low-growing shrubs such as heathers. Among the best for these uses are the *Chamaecyparis lawsoniana* cultivars 'Columnaris', 'Fletcheri', 'Grayswood Pillar', and 'Kilmacurragh'; the 'Skyrocket' and 'Hillii' cultivars of the pencil cedar, *Juniperis virginiana*; and the 'Fastigiata' cultivar of the Irish yew, *Taxus baccata*.

Pendulars

Weeping hybrids and cultivars are often called 'Pendula' or 'Pendulus'. Many are undeniably beautiful but you may find that they tend to give your garden a somewhat fussy appearance unless you use them sparingly – preferably as isolated lawn specimens. The best known pendulous tree, of course, is the weeping willow (*Salix* spp.), but it is unfortunately much too big for most gardens. The following are more likely to suit the proportions of the smaller garden.

CORYLUS AVELLANA is our native hazel, and the weeping form 'Pendula', like the type, is notable for its yellow catkins in early spring and for its bright yellow autumn foliage.

COTONEASTER is a genus that includes a large number of evergreen and deciduous shrubs. 'Hybridus Pendulus', one of the evergreen forms, has strikingly glossy branches forming a cascade and bearing an abundance of bright red berries in the autumn. I find it necessary for the main stem to be trained to a height of 2 m (6 ft) or more to overcome its normally prostrate habit.

PRUNUS includes cherry, plum, peach, and many other ornamental tree species that are particularly attractive as flowering pendulars. Among the best is the 'Kiku-shidare Sakura' cultivar of the Japanese cherry, *P. serrulata*, which has branchlets that droop from arching branches and may grow to a height of 5 m (16 ft). Its double, deep pink flowers, about 4 mm ($1\frac{1}{2}$ in) in diameter, are freely produced in March or April and are followed by glossy green foliage. *P. subhirtella* 'Pendula Rubra' is a slender weeping tree with natural grace and deep coloured flowers – carmine in bud turning to deep rose as they open in late March or early April.

Colourful stems

We tend to assume that the colours of stems and branches are useful mainly in providing a fitting background for the more brilliant tints of flowers, berries and foliage. In fact, many shrubs have very attractively coloured stems, and one of the delights of the winter garden is an unexpected shaft of sunlight picking out the subtle hues and textures of stem bark. I find the best effects are achieved by planting different shrubs with attractive stem colours in groups of five or six. If they are carefully selected, the contrast can be strikingly beautiful. The following select list is grouped according to stem colours.

Red

Cornus alba (red-barked dogwood)
Cornus alba 'Sibirica' (Westonbirt dogwood)
Cornus stolonifera.
Cornus baileyi
Rosa omeiensis pteracantha (Mount Omei rose; shoots bear brilliant, translucent, crimson thorns in the first year)
Salix alba 'Chermesina' (brilliant orange-scarlet)

You will need to cut back hard all the growths of these plants each spring because their brilliant stem colours fade in the second year. Cutting back (sometimes called 'stooling') results in a crowd of wand-like young shoots being thrown up. This process of annual renewal is exhausting, so plants should be fed in summer.

Yellow

Cornus stolonifera 'Flaviramea'
Salix vitellina

These two must also be cut back hard each spring to produce the best winter colour.

The red-stemmed Westonbirt dogwood, *Cornus alba* 'Sibirica', should be cut back in spring for the best winter-bark effect.

White

Rubus biflorus
Rubus cockburnianus

The young stems of these two brambles are covered with an intense white, waxy felt. They will make a striking sight in winter if they are pruned like raspberry bushes, with all old shoots being removed immediately after flowering.

Winter-flowering shrubs

For the shrub garden I define the winter as the period from November to February inclusive. Bear in mind that the flowering months depend to some extent on the region of the country where the shrubs are planted and also on weather conditions, which may differ from one year to the next. However, the lists given below should serve as a generally reliable guide. If you are planting specifically for winter flowers, it may be a good idea to set aside a sheltered corner, perhaps near the front

or back door or the drawing-room window, for this purpose. You will then be more likely to enjoy their colour and scent (many of the shrubs listed are fragrant) and it will be easier to cut a few sprays for indoor use. You can combine your shrubs with a selection from other fine plants that are also winter-flowering – Christmas roses, crocus, snowdrops, iris, and the like.

November

Prunus subhirtella 'Autumnalis Rosea' (autumn cherry; deep rose)
Arbutus unedo (strawberry tree)
Arbutus × andrachnoides (strawberry tree)
Calluna 'Durnfordii' (winter heather; pale pink)
Calluna 'Underwoodii' (pink to silver)
Erica carnea 'Eileen Porter' (winter heath; dark rose pink)
Erica carnea 'Praecox Rubra' (rose red)
Daphne mezereum 'Grandiflora' (mezereon; purple-crimson)

Leycesteria formosa, seen here in summer flower, displays vivid green stems after its leaves fall.

Jasminum nudiflorum (winter jasmine; yellow)
Lonicera fragrantissima (winter honeysuckle; creamy white)
Mahonia × media (yellow)
Viburnum × bodnantense

December

Prunus subhirtella 'Autumnalis' (white)
Erica carnea 'Eileen Porter'
Erica carnea 'Gracilis' (bright pink)
Erica carnea 'Queen Mary' (red)
Erica × darleyensis 'Alba' (white)
Hamamelis mollis (Chinese witch hazel; gold)
Jasminum nudiflorum
Lonicera standishii (creamy white)
Mahonia × media
Viburnum tinus (laurustinus)

January

Camellia sasanqua (white)
Chimonanthus praecox (winter

The Chinese witch-hazel, *Hamamelis mollis*, flowers from December to February.

sweet; straw-coloured)
Crataegus monogyna 'Biflora' (Glastonbury thorn; white)
Erica carnea 'Springwood Pink'
Erica carnea 'Springwood White'
Erica carnea 'Winter Beauty' (rose pink)
Erica carnea vivellii (rich carmine)
Erica × darleyensis 'Darley Dale' (pale pink)
Hamamelis mollis (yellow)
Hamamelis japonica (Japanese witch hazel; yellow)
Lonicera × purpusii (cream)
Viburnum farreri (*V. fragrans*; white)

Camellia sasanqua is the earliest camellia to flower, and does best if it is given the protection of a wall. There are several fine cultivars, with flowers ranging from white and cream, through pink and rose, to deep crimson red. *Chimonanthus praecox* provides one of the finest scents in winter, but may not flower for several years after planting.

The mature plant may be 3 m (10 ft) tall, and prefers a sunny wall site. Its cultivar 'Grandiflorus' has larger and better flowers but less fragrance.

Crataegus monogyna 'Biflora' is a form of the common hawthorn of which, according to legend, Joseph of Arimathea's staff was made (whence its common name: the hawthorns of Glastonbury Abbey are supposed to derive from the planting of Joseph's staff). It flowers in May. *Lonicera × purpusii*, a hybrid of *L. fragrantissima* and *L. standishii*, is a vigorous 2 m (6 ft) bush.

February
Most, if not all, the January selection can be included here to which the following can be added.
Abeliophyllum distichum (white)
Cornus mas (cornelian cherry; yellow)
Daphne mezereum (purple-crimson)
Garrya elliptica (tassel bush; grey-green catkins)
Mahonia japonica (yellow)

Abeliophyllum distichum, a small, twiggy shrub from Korea, has fragrant, tubular blooms somewhat resembling those of forsythia. Borne in side-shoot clusters, they make attractive, long-lasting cut flowers. *Cornus mas*, a large shrub, develops twiggy heads that are lost in their clouds of February blooms. It looks its best if planted against a dark background. *Daphne mezereum* is one of the toughest and most fragrant of winter-flowering shrubs, and its splendidly coloured flowers completely clothe the previous year's shoots. *Note:* the mezereon bears poisonous berries.

Giant leaves

The following are three trees, all of which normally grow to a substantial height, that take well to stooling. The object in cutting them back hard is not merely to reduce them to a size suitable for the smaller garden but to stimulate the development of large, attractively shaped leaves that will contrast interestingly with smaller-scale foliage of the shrubs. All the trees below can safely be cut back to about 2 m (6 ft).

Ailanthus altissima
The Tree of Heaven is one of the best subjects for a smoky atmosphere. Vigorous young shoots produce ash tree-like, pinnate leaves 1 m (3 ft) or more in length made up of 13 to 25 leaflets. The enormous, arching leaves make this a splendid lawn specimen.

Catalpa bignonioides
When stooled the Indian bean tree does not develop its foxglove-like flowers or the 'beans' (fruit) which follow them, but it bears broadly ovate leaves with a heart-shaped base which may be as much as 500 mm ($1\frac{1}{2}$ ft) wide. The leaves are smooth and soft and therefore liable to wind damage, so you should give the tree a sheltered site.

Paulownia tomentosa
The suckers that result from stooling this, the foxglove tree, need to be thinned to a single shoot, which will grow to about 3 m (10 ft) and clothe itself with heart-shaped leaves even larger than those of the catalpa. This tree also should be planted in a warm and sheltered spot.

6 Autumn Colour

THE delights of autumnal colour in the shrub garden come both from fruits and berries and from the colours of the leaves shortly before they fall. The vivid colours of autumn leaves are a result of the mechanism by which deciduous shrubs and trees transfer food products from the leaves to storage tissues in the branches and stems. The mechanism is triggered by the autumn drop in temperature and light intensity. Various chemicals assist in the transfer, notably a substance called anthocyanin, which varies in reaction according to the acid content of the leaves, and gives rise to the glorious golds, oranges, reds, and purples of autumn leaves.

Many gardeners deliberately select plants whose chief or only glory is their autumnal colour, but this practice has its drawbacks. The production of brilliant colours can be disrupted by a variety of weather conditions. If the summer has been very dry, for instance, the leaves will tend to shrivel before achieving their autumnal glory, while early frosts may check the production of anthocyanin. All you can do is to select the most reliable species and cultivars (as listed below) and hope that the clerk of the weather will smile on your efforts.

Acer

Most maples are good for autumn colour and *Acer ginnala* (although it does not have the AGM) is one of the finest in this respect. Its summer dress is of bright green, three-lobed leaves which turn to a spectacular orange and crimson in the autumn. The flowers are inconspicuous but very fragrant. *A. japonicum* has two clones (fixed variants) with the AGM. One of these, 'Aconitifolium', is a hardy, rounded bush from Japan, with leaves divided almost to the base into 9 to 11 lobes. These turn to a rich ruby-crimson in the autumn. The other clone, 'Aureum', is more noted for its delightful lime-green

leaves in summer. *A. palmatum* 'Dissectum', another of the Japanese maples, is perhaps the best of its kind for autumn colour. It forms a low mound, only a few feet high, slowly growing taller and wider. Its leaves are made light and graceful by dividing almost to the base into five to nine lobes which turn to richest red in the autumn. 'Dissectum' needs a moist, well-drained, preferably acid or neutral soil, and a site sheltered from cold winds. *A. palmatum* 'Senkaki', a cultivar of the coral-bark maple, makes a pleasant change in the autumnal scene in that its leaves turn a soft canary yellow.

Amelanchier lamarckii

The snowy mespilus, a multi-stemmed shrub about 4 m (13 ft) high and wide, has two seasons of great beauty. In April, when its pure white racemes expand against a background of half-formed, pink-tinged leaves, it is as fine a sight as the double white cherry. In autumn the leaves turn a rich red, often dappled with a lighter red and yellow. The snowy mespilus is a native of North America and, although it was introduced to Britain more than 200 years ago, it retains the dislike of chalky soils it shares with so many New World shrubs. (In North America, incidentally, it is known variously as the shadbush, service berry, and grape pear.)

Aronia arbutifolia

The red chokeberry of North America is a good 2 m (6 ft) shrub which is not often planted. It flowers in white clusters in April and in autumn bears long-lasting red fruits in conspicuous clusters· and, finally, a riot of exceptionally brilliant red leaves. It needs acid or neutral soils.

Left *Berberis thunbergii*, which grows to a height of about 2 m (6 ft), is one of the best small-garden shrubs for autumn colour. **Right** A magnificent display by *Acer palmatum* 'Heptalobum Osakazuki', one of the finest of the Japanese maples.

Berberis

One of the best of all the barberries for autumnal display, *Berberis thunbergii* forms a low bush about 1 m (3 ft) high. It bears solitary pendant yellow flowers in spring followed by a multitude of bright red berries in the autumn, when its leaves turn brilliant scarlet with a hint of gold. The cultivar *B. thunbergii* 'Atropurpurea Nana' is a more compact form which has blood red foliage during spring and summer and is equally splendid in the autumn. *B. wilsonii* is a most pleasing small shrub of spreading habit with small, soft, green leaves which light up the autumnal scene when they turn to orange and red and blend most attractively with its coral fruits.

Cotinus coggyria

The smoke tree is one of the most desirable of all shrubs, remarkable for panicles which, although bearing few and unremarkable flowers, are made up of branchlets so fine as to resemble silken strands. These are so freely produced in July that the bush seems enveloped in a smoky mist. 'Flame' is the best cultivar for autumn colour.

Cotoneaster

This genus contains some of the most beautiful of the berried shrubs. They will all grow well in most soils and conditions. *C. conspicuus* 'Decorus' is low-growing, about 1 m (3 ft) high, bearing bright red berries, and is excellent as a rock-garden specimen or for covering banks. The 'fish-bone' cotoneaster, *C. horizontalis*, has similar uses; it is especially valuable on north- and east-facing walls owing to the brilliant autumnal colours of both its leaf and berry. *C.* 'Cornubia' is perhaps the most spectacular of the semi-evergreen 4 m (13 ft) hybrids. Its clusters of creamy flowers in June are followed in autumn by arching sprays weighed down by abundant bunches of large-fruited red berries. *C. divaricatus* makes an excellent informal hedge, being one of the most reliable for both dark red fruit and bright autumn colour.

Enkianthus campanulatus

A shrub for lime-free soil in a lightly shaded position, this member of the heather family is a plant of quiet beauty until the autumn, when it assumes a brilliant red and gold cloak.

Boston ivy, *Parthenocissus tricuspidata* 'Veitchii' (often confused with the Virginia creeper) makes a vivid autumn show.

Euonymus alatus

A slow-growing plant some 2 m (6 ft) high and wide, this shrub develops strange corky 'wings' on its branches. The flowers are not conspicuous; the fruits are purplish and split open to show scarlet seeds, but its great merit lies in the brilliant rosy-scarlet autumn foliage. It will succeed in any sunny, well-drained site.

Fothergilla major

A slow-growing shrub best suited to acid soils, *F. major* has broadly ovate leaves, glossy dark green above, which make an admirable foil for the multitude of fragrant, white, bottlebrush-like flowers. In the autumn the leaves change to a remarkable scarlet and gold, sometimes wholly one or the other, sometimes with the scarlet blending subtly into the gold.

Hamamelis mollis

A relative of the above, the Chinese witch hazel is a large shrub (*see* Chapter 5) whose branches are set about from December to February with clusters of sweetly fragrant, golden yellow flowers. The foliage turns yellow in the autumn and makes an admirable foil for the red of most other shrubs.

Oxydendron arboreum

One of the most brilliant large, narrowly upright shrubs for autumn col-our, *O. arboreum* needs the humus-rich, acid soils required by the rhododendrons. I have long been puzzled why this excellent plant, which has been known in this country for over 200 years, is so seldom planted. Its flowers are white and borne in lax panicles in August, when any shrub in flower is welcome. In autumn the foliage turns deep red with tints of crimson and gold. Some deciduous shrubs enchant us in autumn but shed their glorious leaves to form a colourful carpet all too soon. In contrast, *O. arboreum* retains its foliage for many weeks and, indeed, is usually at its best in November.

Parthenocissus

A number of shrubs masquerade under the name of Virginia creeper, but *P. quinquifolia*, introduced from Virginia in 1629, is the genuine article (although since that time botanists have given it five other common names). The plant is a consummate climber and in autumn it clothes many an English wall with a scarlet mantle. One of the other shrubs incorrectly called Virginia creeper is *P. tricuspidata* 'Veitchii' (*Ampelopsis veitchii*), whose authentic common name is Boston ivy. Probably the most widely planted climber in Britain, it is found in almost every town and village in England. It has ovate/trifoliate leaves, readily adapts to a wide range of soils, is very hardy, grows rapidly, and offers a magnificent show of autumn foliage.

Rhododendron luteum

The deciduous rhododendrons are commonly known as azaleas. This one (formerly classified as *Azalea pontica*) is a widely planted and well-loved fragrant yellow azalea – the first of its kind to be introduced. It makes a rather stiff bush up to about 3 m (10 ft) high, bearing crowded clusters of blooms on the ends of the branches each May. In the autumn the attractive, rather narrow green leaves turn to rich shades of crimson, purple, and orange.

Rhus typhina 'Laciniata'

This cultivar of the stag's horn sumach must be treated with some caution, for it is so vigorous that you may have your work cut out preventing it from suckering among your other plants. It is, however, a shrub with most notable and unusually shaped leaves. These can be up to 500 mm ($1\frac{1}{2}$ ft) long if the shoots are cut back to the ground in February each year; they are pinnate – like giant ash leaves – and bring a fern-like appearance to the shrub garden. The autumn colour of mainly orange and yellow is most striking.

Ribes americanum

A member of the flowering-currant family (and very similar to the black-currant of the fruit garden), the American blackcurrant puts on a splendid display in October, when its foliage is a riot of yellow, deep gold, and crimson.

Spiraea prunifolia

Produces delightful arching sprays of double white flowers in May, followed in autumn by orange and red foliage.

Stranvaesia davidiana

This is a vigorous shrub up to 4 m (13 ft) high, bearing dark-green leathery leaves, some of which turn to scarlet from September onwards. Its main attraction is its numerous bunches of drooping scarlet berries, which start to colour up in August. The fruits seem to be bird-proof, and so have a long life. For smaller gardens, *S. davidiana undulata* may be preferred; it is similar in form and colour but about half the size. Both of these have the AGM; so too does *S. davidiana* 'Fructuluteo', which has bright yellow fruits.

Vaccinium corymbosum

The swamp blueberry of North America produces pink-tinted flowers in racemes in May, followed by the blue-black, waxy, edible fruits used to make blueberry pie. The leaves turn brilliant red from September onwards. The plant must have lime-free soil.

Viburnum opulus

One of the many members of this genus to give a noteworthy display each autumn, the guelder rose is taller than most viburnums. It is a native plant whose flowers, in white, flattened heads, brighten the months of June and July, and are followed by bunches of translucent red berries in great abundance which hang on far into the winter. Its pleasant green, maple-like leaves assume brilliant autumn tints.

Right Translucent berries of the guelder rose, *Viburnum opulus*. **Below** The fruit clusters of stagshorn sumach, *Rhus typhina* 'Laciniata', contrast with its brilliant foliage.

7 Climbers and Scramblers

SINCE the heyday of the stately home, with its walled kitchen garden, few householders have built walls specifically for growing plants upon. But house walls, to say nothing of boundary walls and fences, still offer most gardeners the opportunity of indulging their taste for climbing plants. The value of planting against walls is twofold: it gives colour and interest to bare and often unattractive surfaces throughout the year; and it enables you to grow many beautiful plants that are too tender to give of their best in more exposed positions. Even a perfectly hardy plant like the firethorn (*Pyracantha*) flowers and fruits more freely when trained up a wall than when grown as a bush in an open position, especially if you prune it in summer like a fruit tree by shortening new growths.

It is commonly believed that climbers, especially the self-clinging kinds, damage every wall on which they are allowed to grow. I can only say that the experience of 50 years has failed to convince me of this. Nonetheless, one needs to use commonsense in this type of planting. It would obviously be unwise to train climbers up a wall that was in need of pointing or up a plastered structure in which there were cracks that could be enlarged by the plant roots. Many people are also worried that training plants on a house wall invites an invasion of insects and spiders into the home but if the plants are kept well clear of windows, the problem is unlikely to be any worse than normal. Much more important is the need to prevent the climbers from spreading into gutters and under tiles, where they

can cause serious damage. This can be a problem if you have lean-to structures with low gutters and tiles.

Siting

The ground immediately adjacent to a house, especially if it has been recently built, can be a depressing place for plant growth. All too often the builder

has left a concrete footing projecting from the house, and has filled in around the house with building debris. If you are faced with this situation, the only thing to do is to dig out the debris to a depth and width of about 600 mm (2 ft) and replace it with good soil. This is an exhausting chore, but your labours will be rewarded in later years when the plants begin to thrive in these rehabilitated areas. Incidentally, if the debris you have partly removed includes significant quantities of mor-

tar, which is rich in lime, do not plant camellias, rhododendrons, or other acid-loving plants in such areas.

Given the choice, most gardeners would pick a south-facing wall for their plants: it gets more sun and is warmer than other walls. Second best is a west-facing wall; it is preferable to an east wall because the sun is usually warmer in the afternoon than in the early morning. West walls also have the advantage, shared with north walls, of offering plants greater protection against frost in the early spring. Frost damage is due to the morning sun causing the plant tissues to thaw out too rapidly, so rupturing the walls of plant cells. Many plants are killed in this way, and most of the victims are likely to be those planted against east- and south-facing walls, which are the first to be warmed by the morning sun. The danger months are March and April, so plant camellias and other shrubs that flower at this time against west- or north-facing walls.

North walls are commonly regarded as being difficult sites to furnish with plants. This reputation is undeserved. They need a little more thought than other sites, but there are plenty of attractive deciduous and evergreen, flowering and foliage plants that will grow well on north walls. With care and imagination, the north-wall gardener can produce just as attractive a display as his reputedly luckier fellows.

Left *Jasminum nudiflorum* flowers from November to March. **Right** The bright flower-clusters of *Lonicera tragophylla*, a climbing honeysuckle.

Wall shrubs

Early flowers

There can be few garden plants more tolerant than the winter jasmine, *Jasminum nudiflorum*, which is likely to be the earliest to flower on your walls. Its bright yellow flowers erupt along its striking green young shoots from November through to March. It sounds a cheerful note in the garden and is usually prolific enough to be able to spare a sprig or two for vases of winter flowers. Pruning the jasmine is simply a matter of fitting it to the available space; take out large pieces back to the base and avoid shortening the graceful arching branches.

Next to flower might be the delightful *Mahonia japonica*, one of the most rewarding of garden shrubs. Its magnificent, deep-green pinnate leaves, shining and holly-like, make it desirable even when it is not in flower. Then, in the depth of winter, from the end of each shoot it throws a cluster of floral spikes which elongate until they hang in golden chains, each with up to 100 flowers, fragrant with the scent of lily of the valley. Since it will do all this in heavy shade, competing even with the roots of trees and gross feeders such as lilac, it is indeed a paragon among plants.

Another mahonia for which room should always be found is the Oregon grape, *Mahonia aquifolium*, from Canada. Happy in shade, it scrambles about the ground and can be kept down there by pruning; each leaf has five to nine holly-like leaflets of a deep, shining green which may develop a purplish tinge as winter approaches. Spring sees masses of yellow panicles which in the autumn give rise to an abundance of the blue-black berries masked in a grape-like bloom from which it gets its name.

Spring sees the arrival of forsythias such as *F.* × *intermedia* 'Lynwood', of *Camellia japonica* in the guise of a late-flowering cultivar such as *C.* × 'Leonard Messel', and of the superb *Clematis montana rubens*. Later come the large-flowered types such as *Clematis* × *jackmanii*, a rich purple, and the pale mauve *C.* 'Nelly Moser', whose colour is even better on a north wall where it cannot bleach in the sun. The climbing hydrangeas and a honeysuckle such as

Above *Hedera colchia* 'Dentata Variegata', a vigorous scrambling ivy. **Right** The aptly named Oregon grape, *Mahonia aquifolium.*

Lonicera tragophylla – perhaps the brightest yellow among the honeysuckles – will then carry through to the autumn when the berries of the firethorns (*Pyracantha*) and cotoneasters take over.

Many of the best shrubs for north walls are evergreen, so it is wise to plant golden or silver cultivars of the hollies and the ivies to provide colour contrasts in foliage. Among the best hollies for this purpose are *Ilex* × *altaclarensis* 'Golden King' and *I. aquifolium* 'Golden Queen'. Somewhat perversely, the former is a female clone and the latter a male.

Clingers and scramblers

Remarkably few climbers which are really garden-worthy are able to cling without help to a wall or fence. Among those that can are the ivies, notably the natural varieties of common ivy, *Hedera helix*, and Persian ivy, *H. colchica*, which has a handsome variegated variety; all these cling limpet-like by means of aerial roots. The climbing hydrangea, *Hydrangea petiolaris*, is also self-clinging, as is the closely allied *Schizophragma*

Hydrangea petiolaris makes a magnificent self-supporting climber for walls; it may also be used as a scrambler or as a border shrub.

integrifolium, a truly magnificent July-flowering shrub. The only other well-known clingers are the Virginia creeper, *Parthenocissus quinquifolia*, and its relative the Boston ivy, *P. tricuspidata* 'Veitchii', both with marvellous autumn colour (*see* Chapter 6).

The scramblers or smotherers are much more numerous. Many hedgerows carry examples; on chalklands, for instance, you can see *Clematis vitalba*, usually called old man's beard, climbing as high as it can get on the larger hawthorn bushes and then cascading in curtains of magnificent greenish flowers which in autumn turn to the glistening silky foam of seedheads that give rise to its common name. Some of its relatives will grow in the the same way over anything, so beware of planting them near anything you treasure. Many other less vigorous clematis, such as *C. macropetala*, look best when clambering daintily through a cotoneaster or similar shrub by means of their leaf petioles.

In the wild you may also see a honeysuckle, *Lonicera periclymenum*, twining its stems in iron-hard bands around anything in reach. Some of the cultivated varieties will do the same in the garden. The wild-growing species emphasize the fact that many scramblers are fierce colonizers of every available space; some, moreover, are epiphytic – that is, they use other plants for support. It is important to know the characteristics of your scramblers so that you can provide them with suitable support while preventing them from smothering other plants.

Wall supports

There is a multitude of wall support systems. Wallnails and wires placed about 500 mm ($1\frac{1}{2}$ ft) apart are the oldest and simplest method for walls and fences. Another method is to loop narrow strips of canvas or cloth around plant stems and then to nail the ends to the wall.

More expensive alternatives are wooden trellis (probably the most attractive method of all) and plastic-covered steel netting specially made for the purpose. The plastic of the latter is available in various colours. Be careful about choosing your colour; on the face of it, green is the obvious choice, but in many examples it proves to be an aggressive colour that clashes, rather than blends, with foliage; often brown or even black are preferable. The plants' main branches can be attached with tarred twine; green string is better for young growths.

Siting

The following are typical of the wide range of shrubs suitable for wall planting on north- and east-facing and on south- and west-facing sites.

North and east walls

Camellia japonica late-flowering cultivars
Chaenomeles speciosa (Japanese quince)
Clematis montana rubens
Clematis tangutica
Clematis × jackmanii cultivars
Cotoneaster spp.
Euonymus fortunei (*E. radicans*)
Forsythia × intermedia 'Lynwood'
Hedera helix cultivars
Hedera colchica
Hydrangea petiolaris
Jasminum nudiflorum
Kerria japonica 'Pleniflora'
Lonicera tragophylla
Pyracantha spp.

South and west walls

Abelia floribunda (tender)
Abutilon megapotamicum (tender)
Abutilon 'Jermyns' (tender)
Acacia dealbata (silver wattle; tender)
Campsis radicans (trumpet vine)
Camellia × williamsii cultivars
Ceanothus spp.
Chaenomeles spp. (japonicas)
Chimonanthus fragrans (winter sweet)
Choisya ternata (Mexican orange blossom)
Cistus spp. (sun rose)
Clematis spp.
Cytisus battandieri
Desfontainea spinosa (tender)
Garrya elliptica (tassel bush)
Hoheria lyallii (lacebark)
Lonicera spp.
Passiflora caerulea (passion flower; tender)
Prunus triloba (ornamental almond)
Solanum crispum
Teucrium fruticans (shrubby germander; half-hardy)
Wisteria sinensis (*W. chinensis*)

8 Hedges

BROADLY speaking a hedge can be one of two kinds: formal, which in practice means merely that it can be clipped to a specific shape; and informal, which usually implies a flowering hedge of some sort. There is a large number of shrubs that can be used for hedging, but the choice narrows down considerably if you wish your hedge to be beautiful as well as utilitarian. Most would agree that mature, well-clipped yew (*Taxus baccata*) has few if any rivals as a hedge: it is practically impenetrable, has great dignity, and its dark, restful green is a perfect foil for the colour of nearby flowering plants. On the face of it, *T. baccata* seems the perfect hedging plant but in fact it has serious disadvantages, chief among them being its cost and slow growth rate. And you are almost certain to find that other species that seem to have excellent potential as hedges also have practical drawbacks.

Purpose

Obviously, the first thing to decide before choosing your shrubs is the exact purpose of the hedge. Is it to provide shelter for other plants? Is it to frustrate the gaze of inquisitive neighbours? Is it to divide up the garden – separating the compost heap and dustbins, for instance, from the lawn or patio? In terms of decorative effect, does it have to bear flowers? Must it be evergreen, or may it shed its leaves in the winter? And, for the owner of a small garden, the most important question of all: Is there room for a hedge? You will need to allow for a thickness of at least 1.5 m (5 ft) for a formal hedge, and if this is not possible you would be better advised to use a fence planted with climbing shrubs, roses, or the like.

The next question to consider is cost. There are really only two cheap hedging plants that are readily available: privet (*Ligustrum ovalifolium*) and hawthorn or quick (*Crataegus monogyna*). I consider that privet disqualifies itself as a garden hedge on two counts: it needs clipping three or even four times a year, and it robs the soil of nutrients for several yards around its roots. Many people tend to look down their noses at hawthorn because it is by far the most widely used hedge in England and is (or was, until the spread of metal fencing) ubiquitous on our farmlands. I personally regard this as more a recommendation than a drawback. Moreover, hawthorn has many virtues. It is so dense that you cannot see through it even in mid-winter; its new growths in spring are a pleasant deep pink (the colour gives them protection against bright sunlight); and you would probably need to clip it only once a year, in mid-summer. As an important and attractive bonus, the hawthorn is the favourite hedge of our 'smaller native birds.

Cost, however, may not be a decisive factor for the fairly modest lengths of hedging needed in the average garden, so let us have a look at a few alternative plants that fulfil the requirements mentioned.

Formal hedges

These can conveniently be divided into tall and short types.

Tall
Among the conifers the western red cedar, *Thuja plicata*, makes a splendid bright-green hedge, perhaps the best species for thin chalk soils in shaded positions. Like all conifers, it needs to be trimmed for shape and density in early August from the year after planting. Its leaves give off a pleasant scent when handled. The Leyland cypress, *Cupressocyparis × leylandii*, is the quickest-growing garden hedge, commonly adding 600 mm (2 ft) to its height every year. For me it is somewhat lacking in quality, but it is certainly a boon to the impatient gardener. It must be stopped ruthlessly when it approaches the required height. Lawson's cypress, *Chamaecyparis lawsoniana*, makes an attractive hedge and its cultivar, 'Green Hedger', is widely used.

Of deciduous trees, the commonest and best for hedging are hornbeam, *Carpinus betulus*, and beech, *Fagus sylvatica*. They are almost identical as hedges, their most obvious distinguishing feature being that the former has a serrated edge to its leaf and the latter a smooth edge. If you clip them in July there is time for short young growths to develop before autumn, and the leaves, although turning the characteris-

Western red cedar, *Thuja plicata*, makes a superb hedging or screening shrub.

tic golden brown, will stay on all winter. You can give such hedges additional character by including a few purple or copper beeches in the planting at a rate of about one in ten, but placed at random rather than at regular intervals. The famous 'tartan' hedge at Hidcote Manor, Gloucestershire, is a wonderful example of this type.

The best of the hedging hollies is probably *Ilex × altaclarensis*, which with its many variants is commonly known as the Highclere holly. One of its advantages is that the leaves are almost thornless. Five of the cultivars have the AGM; probably the most suitable for hedging are 'Jermyns', with leaves of plain polished green, and 'Lawsoniana', which has beautiful golden variegation.

Short

Low hedges of lavender, *Lavandula spica*, have been used for many hundreds of years in England, and even today few species can compare with it for charm and fragrance. One of the best cultivars is 'Hidcote' (AGM), which bears abundant violet flower spikes in July. You will need to clip it back after flowering to maintain the density of the hedge.

One of the most attractive non-flowering honeysuckles is *Lonicera nitida*, which is usually referred to in the trade simply as 'nitida'. It has been a popular 600 to 900 mm (2 to 3 ft) hedge for many years, but it is so susceptible to damage by snow, playful dogs and children that you would be wiser to use the cultivar 'Yunnan' (often wrongly catalogued as *L. yunnanensis*). This is stouter and more erect in habit and can be clipped into an attractive, durable hedge.

Informal hedges

I mentioned that you will need to allow for a depth of at least 1.5 m (5 ft) for a formal hedge. An informal one will need even more room.

The barberry *Berberis × stenophylla*, which is among the finest of all the evergreen shrubs, is one of the most widely planted for hedging. Quite hardy, it forms a dense hedge up to 3 m (10 ft) high, out of which it throws slender arching sprays about 600 mm (2 ft) long dressed in small, narrow,

Above *Chamaecyparis lawsoniana* hedge. For even growth use vegetatively propagated stock. Below *Lavandula spica* 'Hidcote' hedge. For compactness it must be clipped after flowering.

dark green leaves. In April the sprays are bowed down by a myriad tiny golden-yellow flowers. The hedge must be pruned immediately after flowering. For smaller spaces, two excellent but less vigorous clones are 'Irwinii' and 'Coccinea', with deep yellow and crimson buds respectively. None of these shrubs moves well so it is best to use container-grown plants.

One of the parents of the above hybrid is *B. darwinii*, which also makes a delightful hedge. Of much stiffer habit, it bears small, holly-like leaves about 20 mm ($\frac{3}{4}$ in) long which in spring are almost obscured by a profusion of rich orange-yellow blooms. There is often an attractive harvest of

plum-coloured berries in the autumn.

The spiraeas are not very commonly used for hedging, but they can make an attractive informal division within the garden. One of the best is Foam of May, *Spiraea × arguta*. It is about 1.2 m (4 ft) high and flowers in May on gracefully arching sprays of wood made during the previous year. The flowers are freely clustered on the upper side of the shoots, weighing down the slender fronds in their profusion.

Above Purple and green beech (*Fagus*) hedges retain leaves in winter if clipped in August. Below *Berberis × stenophylla* makes a colourful informal screen if left unclipped.

As they flower on shoots produced the previous season, it is sound practice to cut out some of the oldest shoots right from the base each year after flowering. This encourages movement of food to the young basal growths that will bear flowers next spring.

Planting

The traditional method of planting hedging plants is as a staggered double row. Its only merit is that the hedge looks well-established from the outset. However, shrubs planted in a single row, more widely spaced, soon fill up the gaps. The latter is a better method because it will demand less of the soil later on and is, of course, considerably cheaper because it requires fewer plants. Its only drawback is that the hedge will inevitably appear disappointingly thin during the first few years, while it is becoming established.

It has been said, wisely I think, that hedging plants should be spaced at double the distance recommended by the nurseryman. I am not accusing the nurseryman of dishonesty. It is just that he knows from experience that most gardeners will regard the hedge as far too thin in its first couple of years if it is spaced at the intervals best suited to its maturity.

Buy plants which are bushy and short jointed and have a fibrous root system; these will give a hedge that is well furnished right down to the ground. Firm, moist roots indicate a healthy plant capable of rapid growth. Cut back all damaged roots before planting. Deciduous hedges should be planted in the period from October to March, when they are dormant. Evergreens should be planted in April or May.

The shrubs should be planted at intervals of 300 mm to 1.2 m (1 to 4 ft) depending on their size at maturity. Dig a trench about 600 mm (2 ft) wide and deep to allow for a full spread of the roots. Fork manure or compost into the bottom of the trench, adding about 100 g (4 oz) of bone meal or hoof-and-horn meal for every metre (yard) of trench. Place the shrubs in the centre of the trench, spreading out the roots, and cover them first with fine soil. Then fill with the rest of the soil, firming it well down with your heel. Make sure that the shrubs are at the same soil level as when they were growing at the nursery; you can quite easily distinguish the correct level from the 'tide-mark' left by the nursery soil on the stems. Water thoroughly if the weather is dry.

9 Ground Cover

GROUND cover, is one of the newer gardening terms. It is a simple idea designed to make life easier for the hard-pressed garden owner. If you have ever looked across a heather-clad moorland or into a clump of gorse, or have observed a scramble of blackberries when gathering their fruit, you have seen Nature using ground cover for her own purposes. Very few plants are able to compete with the examples mentioned above. Their vigour is such that they produce complete shade or root dominance to a point where no other plants, or weeds as we might term them, can exist. If you have lily of the valley in your garden, for instance, you will have already come across this total dominance of an area by one kind of plant.

When we introduce ground-cover plants into the garden we are making use of this behaviour to suppress weeds, and in so doing we are saving ourselves a considerable amount of hard work. Awkward banks, spaces at the front of shrub plantings, or simply areas which seem to demand a change of plant texture or habit can be covered by one of the many delightful carpeting plants available instead of being left bare or planted with annuals.

Before discussing these plants, however, I should mention one of their disadvantages. Until the plants touch and intertwine, the soil around them will require as much weeding as in a conventional planting. Nature abhors a vacuum, and weeds, which can be cleared effectively only by hand, will grow freely between newly planted ground coverers. This system may also be more expensive than, say, grass, but over several years it will prove a good investment, in time as well as in money, if labour has to be paid for. When weeding, keep a sharp lookout for young brambles and tree seedlings – oak, ash, sycamore, and others – which if allowed to root deeply are difficult to remove.

Once the ground cover is established, a perfect natural economy exists. The cover prevents excessive baking by the sun, the roots prevent soil-scouring in heavy rain, and the leaf fall provides a natural feeding mulch.

Successful ground cover involves the use of the full range of plants. Apart from shrubs there are many suitable herbaceous subjects such as *Centaurea dealbata* or *Lamium maculatum*, grasses such as *Glyceria aquatica*, and even some ferns. Here I will deal only with shrubs.

Large dense shrubs

Generally speaking, evergreens are best for this purpose. Several *Aucuba* cultivars are excellent and *A. japonica*, the type, has the Award of Garden Merit. Often wrongly called 'laurel', it makes a magnificent dense, rounded bush up to 3 m (10 ft) high and wide, bearing large, broad, deep green leaves. It is male, so if you require red berries in the spring – and these are most attractive – you must plant a female form such as the cultivars 'Longifolia' or 'Hillieri' as well. There is also a smaller female cultivar, about half the size of these, also with the Award of Garden Merit, called 'Nana Rotundifolia'.

The Mexican orange blossom, *Choisya ternata*, is another dense evergreen, quick-growing with trifoliate leaves which are aromatic when crushed. Its flowers are white and, as its common name suggests, most delightfully fragrant when they appear in May.

Cistus × cyprius is a plant for warmer districts only as it can be severely damaged by frost. It grows to about 2 m (6 ft) in height, with narrow evergreen leaves grey-green in colour; its mid-summer flowers consist of 80 mm (3 in) white blooms with blood red blotches at the base of each petal. It scents the air in warm sunny weather.

Other shrubs that will cover an extensive area densely include the following:

Azalea hybrids such as *Rhododendron* 'Arendsii', *R.* 'Haru-no-Kyoki', *R.* 'Hinomayo', and *R.* 'Leo'
Berberis tsangpoensis and *B. wilsoniae*
Camellia 'Lady Clare' and *C.* 'Elegans'
Hebe 'Great Orme', *H.* 'Marjorie', and *H. × franciscana*
Hydrangea macrophylla 'Blue Wave'
Rhododendron 'Britannia', *R.* 'Harvest Moon', and *R. obtusum amoenum*
Viburnum plicatum tomentosum

Viburnum plicatum tomentosum, sometimes called the Japanese snowball tree, forms attractive globular flower heads in May and June. It grows up to 3 m (10 ft) high and wide and is valued not only for its beauty but also as a weed smotherer.

Low growing shrubs

These are the most useful kinds for domestic gardens, for they form a continuous mat in the fashion of heathers on a moorland. There are, indeed, some 50 cultivars of *Calluna*, commonly known as ling or heather, of which about a dozen have an Award of Garden Merit. Among them are the double 'H.E. Beale', originally found wild in the New Forest, which flowers freely in bright pink spikes of up to 250 mm (10 in) long. Another very good double pink is 'H.E. Hamilton' Others include 'County Wicklow', shell pink; 'Alba Plena', double white; and 'Peter Sparkes', deep pink.

Another great family, closely associated with the heathers, is the heaths or ericas. *Erica carnea* is a winter-flowering heath with innumerable cultivars which are equally at home on acid soils or on chalk. 'Springwood White' makes a marvellous carpet; so does 'Winter Beauty', which offers a cheering sight from Christmas onwards. *E. vagans*, the Cornish heath, is a dwarf spreader; one of its cultivars, 'Mrs D.F. Maxwell', bears superb deep cerise flowers. Heaths and heathers as a group have few superiors as carpeters, and with a little care you can select a range of varieties to give flowers in every month of the year.

Spanish gorse, *Genista hispanica*, is one of the best front-of-the-border shrubs, and forms dense undulating hummocks, bright with chrome yellow in June and pleasantly deep green for the rest of the year. If it has a fault it is that individual plants of a group occasionally die for no apparent reason.

Grey makes a pleasant colour contrast. *Santolina chamaecyparissus*, the cotton lavender, is perhaps the most silvery of the greys. Clipped over in March, it remains lightly dwarf and non-flowering.

Lavender, *Lavandula spica*, is not the most weed-proof of shrubs but it will provide reasonable cover if it is clipped in March so that it remains greyer and dwarfer; 'Twickle Purple' and 'Hidcote' are good cultivars.

For sheer quality it would be difficult to beat *Convolvulus cneorum*. Silvery leaved, it bears its white trumpets, pink-flushed without, in May. It needs full sun and good drainage.

As a ground hugger no more than 300 mm (1 ft) high, *Cotoneaster dammeri* is an ideal shrub. It is naturally quite prostrate and rapidly covers a bank or vacant areas in front of or under shrubs. It has dark-green glossy leaves and bears bright red berries in the autumn.

These are just a few examples of the many treasures which can be

Left above Spanish gorse, *Genista hispanica*, forms dense, undulating hummocks, and flowers in June. Left below Several of the evergreen Kurume azaleas make fine ground-cover plants. This one is *Rhododendron* 'Hinomayo'.

pressed into service in the foreground of the shrub border, the place where ground cover is most useful in the small garden. Others include:

Arctostaphylos nevadensis
Arctostaphylos uva-ursi (red bear-berry)
Berberis × stenophylla 'Prostrata'
Cotoneaster 'Hybridus Pendulus'
Cotoneaster 'Skogholm'
Daboecia cantabrica (St Daboec's heath) and cultivars
Euonymus fortunei and cultivars
Gaultheria procumbens (partridge berry)
Hebe albicans
Hebe 'Carl Teschner'
Hebe pinguifolia 'Pagei'
Hypericum calycinum (Rose of Sharon)
Pernettya mucronata and cultivars
Potentilla arbuscula 'Beesii'
Rosmarinus lavandulaceus (tender)
Viburnum davidii
Vinca major (greater periwinkle)
Vinca minor (lesser periwinkle)

Creepers

Certain plants are not capable of developing the stout trunk of a tree or even the substantial branches of a shrub but claim their right to light by climbing up other plants so that they may spread their leaves to the sun.

When deprived of such support some will make a flat mat, like the ivies, and a few others will form a dense thicket by climbing on themselves like the brambles and honeysuckles. Here I shall only describe the best of all these, the ivy. The finest is the Irish ivy, Hedera helix 'Hibernica'. It seems perfectly happy spreading over open ground and has less tendency to climb the nearest tree than other ivies. It bears large, glossy, dark green leaves and has a superbly vigorous constitution. Forms of the common ivy with variegation include H. helix 'Buttercup' (the best gold), 'Marginata' (white-edged), 'Gold Heart' (with a central

splash of gold), and 'Glacier' (the best silver). Although their variegation can add distinction (see Chapter 5), they have not the vigour of the green forms and are best not grown in the shade. H. helix poetica, the Italian ivy, is the brightest green and has yellow fruits when it reaches maturity. A selected form, 'Emerald Gem', is especially

good and has coppery leaves in winter. The Persian ivy, H. colchica, has much larger leaves than any so far mentioned, and in its 'Dentata Variegata' form, with green, cream, grey, and yellow leaves, it is popular and widely planted. I think however that it is a better climber (over a stump or a wall, for instance) than it is a ground coverer.

Right above The lesser periwinkle, Vinca minor, forms a dense evergreen mat that bears its small flowers from March to July. Right below Irish ivy, Hedera helix 'Hibernica', a rampant grower, is excellent for ground cover if denied support of another plant.

10 Seaside Gardens

GARDENERS who live on or very near the coast know that such areas provide rather special conditions for raising plants. A substantial stretch of salt or fresh water retains its warmth for longer than does land. The practical consequence of this is that, as a general rule, coastal strips up to half a mile wide or more enjoy air temperatures a degree or two higher than those of areas farther inland. This makes a whole range of shrubs grow better, and earlier, in coastal regions than elsewhere; more to the point, it enables many seaside gardeners to grow plants of doubtful hardiness (fuchsias, for example) that would succumb to conditions in neighbouring areas only a few miles inland.

This, as they say, is the good news. But seaside gardening also presents various difficulties, mainly to do with providing adequate shelter for plants. Many of our worst storms sweep in from the sea. Of course, such storms may, and often do, penetrate far inland; but by then much of their strength may have been dissipated by hills. The coastal garden, however, will have borne the brunt of wind and rain. Moreover, at the seaside the wind may be carrying salt sea spray, which is a deadly enemy of most shrubs; it may also be carrying sand particles whipped up from dunes, and these can inflict a physical battery that few plants can survive.

Many seaside gardeners will not need reminding of the havoc that can be caused by such storms. The immediate physical evidence of damage caused by salt spray usually looks no worse than that caused by ordinary rainwater but the soaking of plant wounds with salty water leads to chemical changes that can do lasting, often irreparable harm.

Filter fences

The answer to this problem is to provide a means of filtering the wind, and the best method is some form of semi-permeable fencing. 'Semi-permeable' is the key word here, for it explains why a fence is better than a wall in these circumstances. A wall, or other solid barrier, would force the wind to go round or over it and would set up vortices and other turbulence on the far side which could create more havoc than if the gale was allowed to run free. On the other hand, experiments have shown that a semi-permeable fence will greatly reduce wind speeds, will create far less turbulence than a solid wall, and will protect a stretch of garden more than 20 times longer than the fence height. It has been demonstrated that the best of such fences present a surface consisting of 60 per cent solid matter (wood or plastic) and 40 per cent aperture; I personally have built many wind-break fences in which the proportions are about 50–50 and have found them quite satisfactory.

The type of fencing you choose depends on how important appearance is. The most readily available is likely to be plaited wattle. It is really too solid, but you may be able to put in a special order for 50–50 spacing. The commonest forms of chespale (chestnut pales secured top and bottom with wires) have about three parts space to one part solid at best, so if you choose one of these you will need to ask the manufacturer for a supply made up with spaces the same width as the pales he is using. The best-looking fencing is a structure using 25 mm (1 in) wide vertical slats carried on horizontal bars of 50 mm (2 in) square section supported by suitable posts. A 25 mm (1 in) space should be allowed between each slat.

Left *Escallonia* 'Edinensis' is one of many cultivars of this genus adapted for seaside gardens. Right The sea buckthorn, *Hippophae rhamnoides*, is probably the toughest seaside shrub and makes an excellent windbreak.

An excellent filter fence can be made with pales and spaces of equal width.

Natural protection

If you are fortunate enough to have room to spare, the wind-filtering task can be carried out by a hedge. Remember though, that even with intensive planting the hedge will take some years to reach a sufficient density to offer adequate protection. Bear in mind, too, that if you live in an especially exposed seaside position, the tough and admittedly somewhat unlovely plants you will be obliged to use will need to attain a height of perhaps 3 m (10 ft).

The plants will have to grow under hostile conditions, so they are entitled to the best ground preparation you can manage. Ideally, double dig, and add humus copiously; if the area is of any size you may have to use mechanical cultivation, perhaps by contract. At all events, ensure that the supply of humus is worked in, and add at least 100 g/m² (4 oz/sq yd) of a slow-acting fertilizer such as bone meal.

Seaside shrubs

The following shrubs all merit consideration when you are planning your wind-break.

Tamarix These excellent wind-resisters have slender graceful branches and feathery foliage tipped with exquisite pink plumes as much as 300 mm (1 ft) long. The best of them – and they deserve a place in the garden proper as well as in the wind-break – are the spring-flowering *Tamarix tetandra* and *T. parviflora*, both of which flower on shoots made the previous summer. In the shelter belt prune them sparingly, as the object is to obtain a mass of shoots to act as a wind filter; in the garden, prune them back hard soon after flowering in May or June to allow as long a period as possible for the new young flowering shoots to grow. Flowering later in the summer is *Tamarix pentandra*, which blooms on current season's wood in August, and therefore can be pruned in winter. Good later-flowering shrubs are so rare that this one deserves a place in every garden.

If I had to choose one shrub which would for certain survive no matter what the exposure, I think I would choose the sea buckthorn, *Hippophae rhamnoides*. This will grow on the very edge of the sea, with nothing more sustaining than a sand dune to nourish it. Although it is gaunt in winter, in the summer it dons its silvery willow-like leaves; and in autumn, if you have planted male and female forms, it festoons its boughs with a superabundance of golden-orange berries. As they age, these berries emit the unpleasant odour of stale beer, so do not pick stems for a winter vase; and

remember, when pruning near them, that the yellow stain from the berries defeats most of the usual fabric-cleaning fluids.

The common gorse, *Ulex europaeus,* is 'common' only in the sense that there are few places where it will not grow. Its all-the-year-round flowering has been acknowledged in a country saying, 'When the gorse is out of blossom, kissing's out of season'; but it is at its finest in late summer. Golden acre upon golden acre, sometimes patchworked by heather and framed by a blue sea, it is one of our most indispensable natives. If you use it in your windbreak, plant container-grown specimens complete with their growing mixture, because gorse responds unfavourably to root disturbance. Alternatively, raise it from seeds sown where it is to grow.

In contrast, I suppose the evergreen tree purslane, *Atriplex halimus,* is about the dullest protective plant but although it is a sober grey in colour it earns its keep by its exceptional toughness. It rarely tops 1.5 m (5 ft), but it grows rapidly. Indeed, it is possibly the best shrub for a really quick-growing hedge behind which other plants may be established.

From New Zealand comes the unromantically named wire-netting plant, *Muehlenbeckia complexa,* a rampant climber in southern England that will cheerfully swamp a wooden fence or other plants to form an impenetrable thicket. Its growth consists of thin, black, wiry stems (whence its common name) on which are borne tiny, often violin-shaped leaves. It seems quite indifferent to the elements and makes an admirable wind filter on its own.

There are many other familiar plants that can be included in a wind-break. It is always a good idea to select those species that grow freely in the wild state in your area – you can then be confident that they will thrive in your garden. Typical examples are sycamore, *Acer pseudoplatanus,* which will need to be cut back almost to the ground every year or so to produce a thicket of young shoots; elderberry, *Sambucus nigra*; willow, *Salix caprea*; sloe, *Prunus spinosa*; and white poplar, *Populus alba*. A thicket made up of some or all of these will provide shelter within which other, more unusual plants may flourish.

Special adaptations

Many plants have evolved in ways that aid their survival in inhospitable places. Familiar examples include the adaptations that equip cacti for life in deserts, and water-lilies, with their root system entirely below water. So it is no surprise that some plants are especially well fitted to withstand seaside gales.

It is well known that grey-leaved plants do well beside the sea. 'Greyness' is often due to an extra covering on the surface of the leaf. Many of the shrubby senecios, notably the hybrid *S.* 'Sunshine' (frequently catalogued as *S. laxifolius*), have a covering of hairs which can be (but should not be) rubbed off; others, including *S. monroi,* grow a thick underfelt which gives added protection to the internal tissues of leaves. In other plants, including mesembryanthemums and dianthus, greyness is due to a waxy coating resembling the bloom on a grape. Another device, found in *Escallonia rubra* and *E. macrantha,* involves covering the leaf surfaces with a sticky substance.

Leaves are especially prone to damage by wind and rain, and some plants have dispensed with leaves in the usually accepted form and have transferred their food-producing activities to green shoots, which present a smaller surface area to the elements. Typical of such plants are the common gorse, already mentioned, and Spanish gorse, *Genista hispanica.* Alternatively, plants may retain their leaves but evolve a two-layered epidermis (protective cell-surface structure), as in *Hebe* species, or make it specially tough, as in *Euonymus japonica.*

All these plants will thrive at the seaside, and some at least are worthy of inclusion in the garden proper rather than in the wind-break. Others useful in the protective barrier include hawthorn, *Crataegus oxycantha; Griselina littoralis;* boxthorn, *Lycium chinense;* and the tamarisks *Tamarix anglica* and *T. gallica.*

Seaside favourites

The following, although lacking special adaptations, are attractive shrubs that

Above left Common rosemary, *Rosmarinus officinalis,* makes an excellent seaside shrub. If used as an informal hedge it should be lightly pruned after it has flowered in May.
Above Gorse is well able to withstand seaside winds. *Ulex europaeus* 'Plenus', a double form of common gorse, makes a compact garden hedge and flowers throughout the year.

are widely used within gardens, rather than in wind-breaks, at the seaside.

Cistus palhinhae, C.×cyprius, C. ×purpureus, and *C.×laurifolius.*
Elaeagnus pungens 'Maculata'.
Escallonia 'Edinensis', *E.* 'Peach Blossom', and *E.* 'Donard Seedling'.
Fuchsia magellanica 'Gracilis', *F. magellanica* 'Riccartonii', and *F.* 'Mrs Popple'.
Hebe 'Carl Teschner' (veronica) and *H.* 'Great Orme'.
Hydrangea (many cultivars).
Rosmarinus officinalis (rosemary).
Santolina chamaecyparissus (cotton lavender).
Spartium junceum (Spanish broom).
Ulex europaeus 'Plenus'.

11 Problem Soils

I HAVE lost count of the number of occasions when I have come across inexperienced gardeners who have gone to endless trouble, and often considerable expense, in unsuccessful attempts to adapt their gardens to the needs of particular plants. The problem, in the great majority of cases, has lain in trying to persuade plants to grow in soil that is quite unsuited or even hostile to their needs. The solution, at least in general terms, is to grow only those plants that will thrive in your soil.

Chalk and limestone

Having gardened on the South Downs for over 40 years, I have come to terms with the severe restrictions placed on the gardener by soil containing large quantities of free lime. He cannot, for instance, grow some of the most popular shrubs, such as azaleas, rhododendrons, camellias, and certain of the heathers. I shall not encourage you to try using raised beds, chemical treatments, or the other dodges sometimes recommended for dealing with chalky soils; they nearly always fail owing to infiltration of lime or to the presence of lime in the water supply (most tap water in chalky areas is quite strongly alkaline). Since there are so many good plants which thrive on these limy soils, it seems sensible to use them. There is no reason why you should not grow, say, a camellia in a very large pot or tub filled with acid soil and peat, if you can water it with rain water.

The acidity scale

The acid or lime content of soils is represented on what is called the *p*H scale. The scale runs from 1 to 14. A *p*H reading of 7 corresponds to a neutral soil – one that is neither acid nor alkaline. Above that figure the soil is increasingly alkaline, up to a maximum of about 8.5; below 7 the soil is increasingly acid to a lowest (maximum acidity) reading of about 3.5. Inexpensive measuring kits enabling you to make your own readings are available from horticultural stores.

It is important that you have accurate readings on your own site: it is quite possible that the soil in a neighbour's garden a few doors down the street is different from yours, so do not rely on his readings. Most shrubs enjoy a *p*H of 5.7 to 6.7, and if your soil falls into this range you will have few worries. If it has a lower *p*H you will have to concentrate mainly on acid-lovers, such as ericaceous plants. There are quite a few shrubs that are indifferent to *p*H factors, notably barberries, cistus, and hibiscus. The following are some of the most important shrubs that should not on any account be planted on soils with a *p*H more than 7:

Azaleas
Calluna spp. (heathers, ling)
Camellia spp.
Daboecia spp. (heaths)
Erica (heaths) except winter-flowering species
Gaultheria spp. (partridge berry)
Halesia spp. (snowdrop tree)
Kalmia spp. (calico bush)
Magnolia spp.
Nyssa spp.

Pernettya spp.
Pieris spp.
Rhododendrons
Spiraea × *billiardii*
Spiraea douglasii
Vaccinium spp. (blueberry, etc)

The *p*H reading also indicates the availability of soil nutrients to plants. At the optimum reading of 5.7 to 6.7 the plants can absorb all the major elements necessary to their growth. Above and below these readings the availability of these elements decreases steadily and some of the minor but still necessary elements may be almost unobtainable. Lack of elements such as calcium, manganese, and iron gives rise to unhealthy growth, yellow leaves, and other signs of distress.

Improving alkaline soils

The only way to improve alkaline soils is to add as much organic matter as possible. Garden compost is excellent; even better is peat as it usually has a *p*H of about 4.5, which should bring a high *p*H down nearer to neutral. Good alternatives include leaf mould or manure, if you can get either; seaweed if you are near the coast and can stomach the smell; and spent hops from the local brewery, or spent mushroom compost. You can even rot down straw (though this will take up to a year to decompose thoroughly). All these materials must be dug into the soil to a depth of about 350 mm (14 in). Composting is not, of course, a permanent solution: unless it is repeated annually

Magnolias, such as this *M. soulangeana* 'Alba Superba', thrive on heavy soils.

the soil will reassume its natural alkalinity. Moreover, many of these materials are expensive, and most gardeners will have to content themselves with improving only part of the garden.

Chlorosis

Few who garden on alkaline soils escape trouble with this disorder. A plant in apparently good health starts to produce pale green leaves, usually at the tips of young shoots; soon the leaves turn yellow and then white. Part or the whole of the plant may suffer. The worst-affected plants will die; others may continue to live in permanent ill-health.

Chlorosis is due to a breakdown of the systems which produce the leaf pigment, chlorophyll. Since this pigment plays a central role in photosynthesis, the process by which a plant uses the energy of sunlight to make its food, chlorosis can be said to have the effect of starving a plant. Its cause is not precisely understood, but is thought to be linked with high alkalinity preventing the plant absorbing iron and manganese, which are essential to normal growth; certainly soils lacking these two elements produce symptoms typical of chlorosis. (Lack of magnesium, which is commonly deficient on chalk soils, produces quite different symptoms.)

Can chlorosis be cured? The short answer is, no. There is, however, a number of proprietary chemicals based on chelated iron that will restore shrubs to something like normal growth, but their effect is to check or mask the trouble rather than to cure it. Usually the chemicals will need to be applied once a year, and they are all rather expensive. In short, it seems to me that the only sensible course is to avoid planting susceptible shrubs on highly alkaline soils – that is, soils having a pH greater than 8. Shrubs especially prone to chlorosis are:

Ceanothus caeruleus (*C. azureus*)
Ceanothus 'Gloire de Versailles'
Chaenomeles spp. (japonicas)
Escallonia spp. and cultivars
Hydrangea macrophylla
Magnolia spp.
Prunus laurocerasus
Skimmia japonica
Spiraea japonica
Stephanandra incisa
Weigela florida

Sandy soils

Sandy soils, arid slopes, and gravelly soils present problems which are too great for the majority of the shrubs we normally depend on. However, there are a number, some of great beauty, which not only thrive in these seemingly inhospitable soils but even succeed better there than in ordinary soils.

Let us not forget also that sandy soils are a cultivator's dream. They are easily dug, they are easy to supply with humus, and they warm up quickly and are therefore 'early'. The reverse of the coin is that they are hungry soils, needing constant feeding and mulching, and that they drain easily, and are therefore liable to run short of water very quickly. An automatic watering system on these soils is a great boon but is expensive. It is usually cheaper to install taps at convenient points in the garden so that watering by can is not too onerous a job. In general, plant small, mulch well, and do not allow the soil to dry out. In this way a good root system can be built up in the first year which will stand the plants in good stead if drought occurs.

Shrub selection

There can be few better shrubs for sandy soils than the sun roses, *Cistus*. *C.* × *cyprius* was given the AGM more than 50 years ago. It grows rapidly to a 2 m (6 ft) high bush in a few years. Its flowers are borne in clusters, each one with five white petals around a golden central boss ringed by blood-red imprints at the base of each petal. *C.* × *purpureus* is somewhat similar except that the flowers are rosy-crimson with chocolate-coloured basal blotches. Probably the hardiest is *C.* 'Silver Pink', a well-named hybrid which makes attractive hummocks some 1 m (3 ft) high. Its long clusters of pastel-shaded flowers look best against a dark background.

On sandy banks the double-flowered gorse, *Ulex europaeus* 'Plenus', makes a

Below A lime-loving dwarf shrub, the mezereon, *Daphne mezereum*, flowers in March and April. **Right above** *Cytisus* × *purpureus*, a sun rose, is a favourite for dry, sandy soils. **Right below** St Dabeoc's heath, *Daboecia cantabrica*, is an attractive dwarf shrub for acid soils.

fine show. It is smaller than the common gorse, forming a dense, rounded bush about 1.5 m (5 ft) high; evergreen in winter, it gives its best display in April to May, when it is submerged in a glory of double chrome-yellow flowers. If you prefer flowers in the autumn, try *Ulex gallii*, which will cover its dark green mounds with golden yellow flowers mainly between August and October. You can rely on it not exceeding its allotted space. The Spanish gorse, *Genista hispanica*, makes rolling hummocks 500 mm (1½ ft) high which are covered with golden yellow at mid-summer.

Other good shrubs for sandy soils include:

Berberis spp. (barberries)
Calluna vulgaris and cultivars
    (heathers, ling)
Colutea arborescens (bladder senna)
Cotoneaster spp.
Erica (heaths)
Genista spp. (broom)
Helianthemum spp.
Hibiscus spp.
Kerria spp.
Lonicera spp. (honeysuckle)
Santolina spp. (cotton lavender)
Tamarix spp. (tamarisk)
Teucrium fruticans (shrubby germander)

Clay soils

I have dealt with methods of cultivating the most intractable clay soils in Chapter 2: improving drainage, adding humus regularly, and surface planting are the salient points. There are, in fact, many shrubs that will thrive in such seemingly inhospitable mediums, notably species of the following genera:

Abelia	*Hypericum*
Aucuba	*Mahonia*
Berberis	*Magnolia*
Chaenomeles	*Philadelphus*
Choisya	*Potentilla*
Cotinus	*Pyracantha*
(smoke bush)	*Rhododendron*
Cotoneaster	(acid clays only)
Cytisus	*Skimmia*
Deutzia	*Spiraea*
Escallonia	*Symphoricarpos*
Forsythia	(snowberry)
Genista	*Viburnum*
Hamamelis	*Weigela*
(witch hazel)	

12 Rhododendrons and Azaleas

APART from the rose, the rhododendron and its relatives are probably the most popular plants grown by the amateur gardener. A liking for rhododendrons can easily develop into a passion, and many gardeners spend their lives happily exploring the ramifications of this enormous family. At least 500 species are grown in Britain, and of the making of hybrids and cutivars there is no end. The vast majority flower in April and May, but some bloom as early as January and others as late as August. Few people have gardens large enough to accommodate anything like a representative selection of rhododendrons and azaleas. If you are planning to grow them, try to visit one of the many great collections of these plants in Britain. This will enable you to get some practical knowledge of the enormous variety available – especially in terms of size, growing habit, and colour – from which you can make a short list of types that are suitable for your garden.

Most of our rhododendrons and azaleas come from the vast jumble of mountain valleys of the eastern Himalayas, western China, and northern Burma. Here they flower and make their growth in the wet, misty monsoon season. This is followed by heavy snow, which protects the plants through the winter and supplies them with ample water as it melts in the spring. Although we are often advised to try to simulate a plant's natural growing conditions when we grow it in our garden, it is just about impossible in this case, and we are fortunate that

the rhododendrons are sufficiently tolerant not to demand it.

Nearly all the Ericaceae family (which includes the azaleas and rhododendrons) are lime-hating. Before planting make sure that the pH (acidity) of your garden soil is 6.5 or less. Ensure, too, that your water supply does not come from an alkaline source.

Check with your local water department on this, for sooner or later you will have to water and you might give your plants weak limewater without realising it.

In general, all acid soils can be treated to suit rhododendrons; the most difficult types are perhaps the clays. The methods used are as described in Chapter 2 except that if you wish to

use spent mushroom compost, you must make sure that chalk has not been used in the casing (it can usually be seen as white fragments). Also, if you are making compost yourself, omit the scattering of lime that is usually applied between the layers of garden waste.

Mature garden soils, especially in an old vegetable garden, should be regarded with suspicion as they are likely to have been heavily limed in the past. Moreover, their crumbly soil structure is not liked by the roots of young rhododendrons and azaleas.

It is often said that rhododendrons are shallow rooted. Undoubtedly their feeding roots are near the surface, but if they are given a well-prepared site their anchor roots will go deep and provide both stability and food which will be greatly to the plants' advantage when there is a drought. So cultivate deeply before planting, adding copious supplies of humus.

Where to plant

Light woodland is generally considered to be the best environment for rhododendrons and azaleas, so try to arrange light shade among the existing plants and buildings. Some rhododendrons from monsoon countries have very large leaves and these require the shadiest spots, but most will grow cheerfully if they are protected by a wall and are lightly shaded by an existing tree. Do not plant directly into

Left A young *Rhododendron yakushimanum*, a hardy, sun-loving, and much admired species. **Right** *R. obtusum* 'Kaemferii', a dwarf evergreen azalea, flowers abundantly in May.

the area dominated by the tree's main root system, or your plants will be starved of water and food. Some large shrubs, such as the snowdrop tree (*Halesia*) and *Cornus* will give satisfactory shade for the smaller species and hybrids. Do not, however, fall into the trap of assuming that rhododendrons must have deep shade: most of them resent it, and given the choice of full sun or deep shade they will, I think, prefer the former.

Rhododendrons and azaleas are accommodating plants in that their tight root systems make them easy plants to move. The best time to do this is in early autumn, when the soil is still warm and there is a prospect of moist weather ahead.

How to plant
Deep planting is to be avoided in view of the plants' surface-rooting habit. The root ball should be at soil level with a light covering of peat or other humus. Some gardeners like to leave a shallow depression around the stems to aid watering in the early years but on heavy soils you should build a low mound; you will then have to stake the plants. It is vital that the mounds are not allowed to dry out. The larger rhododendrons should be spaced about 3 m (10 ft) apart, and azaleas about half that distance.

After-care
Spread mulch on the soil around the plants to conserve moisture, control weeds, and provide a secondary supply of food. Good mulches for rhododendrons and azaleas are beech or oak leaf mould, pine or spruce needles, peat, and bracken fronds; shredded bark is also excellent if you can get it. Do *not* mulch with grass mowings, rotting straw, farmyard manure, or other materials that could become soggy and impervious to air while rotting. Rhododendrons and azaleas are not heavy feeders, but in their early years you should give them a light dressing – say, 30 g/m² (1 oz/sq yd) – of a low-nitrogen complete fertilizer to promote good growth.

Young plants should not be allowed to flower too freely, so reduce buds to one per shoot.

No pruning of the mature plants is necessary, but it is sound practice to remove the dead heads of flowers; this will prevent them from setting seed, which drains the plants of vigour. Break off the dead heads with finger and thumb, taking care not to damage the young growths which are often immediately below.

Choosing your plants
Often the first question the inexperienced gardener asks is: What is the difference between rhododendrons and azaleas?

Botanically, both belong to the genus *Rhododendron*, but usually the common name rhododendron is applied to the evergreen species and azalea to the deciduous species. This distinction is not, however, completely rigorous: the Japanese azaleas, which are familiar as pot plants at Christmas-time, are evergreen or at least semi-evergreen.

A more important problem for the gardener unfamiliar with these plants is how to select, from the bewildering array of species, hybrids, and cultivars listed in the specialist catalogues, a range of rhododendrons and azaleas suitable for his particular garden. The average gardener will want to avoid the larger plants, for many species can attain a height and width of 12 m (40 ft) or more. He will also want to select reliable hardy species, remembering that most of these plants are native to regions much warmer than Britain. All the plants in the following selection meet these needs; moreover they bear the imprimatur of the AGM, so they can be relied upon to be of a high all-round quality.

Species

The following introductions from the wild have been steadily improved by selecting only the very best types for propagation.

R. calostrotum is a small species no more than 1 m (3 ft) high and is one of the most beautiful for the rock garden. It flowers freely when very young, its bright rosy-crimson blooms completely covering the bush. It has a highly regarded cultivar, 'Gigha', which bears deep claret-red flowers.

R. luteum, the common yellow azalea (but not to be scorned on that account), usually reaches about 3 m (10 ft) in height and width. It has one of the most superb fragrances of any flower in the garden, and in autumn it is ablaze with colourful leaves.

R. obtusum 'Amoenum' is a dwarf evergreen azalea rarely more than 1.5 m (5 ft) in height but sometimes much wider. It flowers with immense freedom in May, when its brilliant magenta blooms are apt to make a colour clash with other plants. For this reason, many gardeners plant it in a solitary position.

R. scintillans, which attains a height of about 1 m (3 ft), is regarded by some horticulturalists as among the best of all small shrubs. Its flowers vary in colour from lavender to royal blue. Buy the FCC (First Class Certificate) form if you can; it is usually identified as such in nurserymen's catalogues. It is as near blue as you are likely to find, and is very hardy – even its flowers are frost-resistant.

R. yakushimanum. This would be the choice of many people if they were allowed only one rhododendron. It makes a dome-shaped bush clothed in dark green leaves over which each May come the bell-shaped trusses, pale shell pink ageing to pure white. It grows to 1.5 m (5 ft).

Hardy hybrids

These hybrids are the result of deliberate crosses, and most of them date from the 19th century. They have qualities of hardiness, generous foliage, and robust flower trusses capable of standing up to the worst weather.

R. 'Britannia' is of Dutch origin, in spite of its name, and is one of the most popular of this group. Of superb habit, it forms a compact bush about 2 m (6 ft) high. The bell-shaped flowers, each about 80 mm (3 in) wide, are a glowing scarlet. It is perhaps the best hardy hybrid of this colour.

R. 'Cynthia' is characterized by huge pyramidal trusses of magenta-pink flowers 80 mm (3 in) wide. It has one of the sturdiest constitutions and has been widely planted for more than 100 years. Make sure you see the colour before you buy, as it needs careful harmonizing.

R. 'Fastuosum Flore Pleno', first raised in Belgium in the 1840s, is still

highly regarded. It is a large, compact shrub carrying broad, lax trusses blue-mauve in colour. One of the hardiest in this group.

R. 'Loder's White' is the largest plant recommended in this section; it will usually attain a height of at least 4 m (13 ft). I include it because of its exceptional quality. It bears huge, pure white flower trusses set against handsome dark-green foliage.

R. 'Mrs Charles E. Pearson' has superb icy mauve flowers, 100 mm (4 in) wide, with 10 to 12 flowers in each truss.

R. 'Pink Pearl' is probably the best-known hardy hybrid. It bears soft pink flowers that later acquire a mauve hue, which somewhat detracts from their charm. Very free-flowering, it is also tough and hardy.

R. 'Purple Splendour' bears the most sumptuous royal purple flowers, up to 15 in each truss. It flowers late (early June), is compact, and of medium size.

R. 'Sappho' is a fine, free-growing bush, well liked for more than a century. The large trusses of flowers are white with a flared stain of purple.

Deciduous azalea hybrids

This group of azaleas will set your garden ablaze from early May to late June. It is hard to think of a desirable quality they do not possess: they are quite hardy (save that in a few cases early growth can be frosted); they are virtually trouble-free on typical acid soils; they will grow in full sunlight; many are fragrant; and most have superb autumn leaf colour. All this and, of course, beautiful flowers that range in colours from the most delicate pastel shades to riotous reds, oranges, and scarlets.

These deciduous hybrids can conveniently be divided into various types which are the result of hybridization mainly in Europe, America, and New Zealand over the last 150 years or so.

Mollis azaleas
This type is the earliest, flowering in early May. Their large and unfortunately scentless flowers, which appear before the leaves, give brilliant dis-

Rhododendrons in a woodland setting.

plays of orange, flame, and scarlet. Most of them are 1.5 m (5 ft) in height. Of more than 20 with the AGM, *R.* 'Spek's Orange' and *R.* 'Dr M. Oosthoek', a deep orange-red, are especially good; but all the others are of high quality, and you are unlikely to be disappointed even if you buy seedlings in the mixed colours that are offered by many firms.

Knap Hill hybrids

These follow the Mollis into flower. The first of the type came from the great firm of Waterer at its Knap Hill Nursery in Surrey. Many distinguished additions to the range have been made by the Rothschilds at their gardens at Exbury, Hampshire (they are sometimes grouped separately as 'Exbury Azaleas'), while more recent work in New Zealand has extended the range even farther.

It seems strange that none of this hybrid type has received the Award of Garden Merit, but this serves to emphasize the fact that the quality of these azaleas is so high that it is not possible to identify any as being outstandingly better than the others. Indeed, it is common practice for garden centres to offer seedlings sold simply by colour; these represent very good value.

Orange, flame, crimson, and rose are the predominant colours of Knap Hill hybrids, and their height rarely exceeds 2 m (6 ft). Those I find especially attractive include *R.* 'Silver Slipper', pale pink/white with yellow blotches; *R.* 'Gibraltar', orange; *R.* 'Knap Hill Red', and *R.* 'Berryrose', salmon pink with a yellow eye. But there are many other superb examples.

Ghent azaleas

We are indebted to the work of a Belgian baker of Ghent around 1820–30 for this group of deciduous hybrids. It is remarkable that one of his originals, *R.* 'Coccinea Speciosa', which has the AGM, remains one of the most

Left above *R.* 'Loder's White' has been described as the finest hybrid rhododendron ever raised. It makes a large plant, is relatively hardy, and attains its purest colour when grown in light shade. **Left below** *R.* 'Speks Orange' is a spectacular deciduous hybrid that flowers later in May than most other Mollis azaleas.

popular of this group. Other beautiful examples of the type that also have the AGM are *R*. 'Narcissiflorum', with pale yellow double flowers, and *R*. 'Corneille', which has cream and pink flowers.

In general the Ghents are smaller-flowered than the Mollis and Knap Hill hybrids, although this does not detract from their garden quality. They are superbly fragrant and brilliantly coloured in the autumn, none more so than *R*. 'Corneille'.

Evergreen azalea hybrids

There are several different types of evergreen azalea hybrids, but I shall confine my remarks mainly to the best known and most popular, the Kurume azaleas. These outstanding hybrids take their name from a city on Japan's southernmost island of Kyushu, where they were first developed. They were introduced to Europe by the noted plant hunter E.H. ('China') Wilson, who in 1918 made a selection of the 50 he considered to be the best. The hardiest of these are still available today. They enjoy full sun and moist roots and they flower, principally in May, with the utmost freedom. All are about 1 m (3 ft) high or a little more, and the following five – all of which have the AGM – are among the finest:

R. 'Azuma-kagami' (deep pink, double)
R. 'Hinodegiri' (bright crimson)
R. 'Hinomayo' (clear pink)
R. 'Kirin' (deep rose)
R. 'Kure-no-yuki' (white).

Two other azalea hybrids of a quite different type, both with the AGM, are also well worth growing. They grow to a height of about 1.5 m (5 ft) and bear much larger flowers than the Kurume type:

R. 'Palestrina' (pure white flowers with a green eye)
R. 'Vuyk's Scarlet' (bright red).

Right above *R*. 'Palestrina' is a most distinctive evergreen azalea hybrid, providing an oasis of reticent colour and form in the rhododendron border. **Right below** One of the original Ghent azaleas, *R*. 'Coccinea Speciosa' has been popular for almost 150 years. Although smaller-flowered than many other azaleas, the Ghents are richly scented.

13 Pruning and Propagation

WHY prune? After all, nobody prunes plants in the wild, yet few gardeners could hope to improve upon the superabundance of flowers produced by gorse on our open heathlands. Why cannot the gardener also let nature take its course? The answer is that pruning of a sort *does* occur in the wild: we call it the survival of the fittest. Gorse seedlings compete with other gorse seedlings; the stronger deny light and food to the weaker, which soon die out. Later, competition begins between the shoots of the surviving gorse plants; usually it is the ones in the heart of the bush which succumb, because they lack light.

This natural 'pruning' helps plants to survive in the wild, but it does not necessarily result in plants that are acceptable in the garden. As well as to speed the process of natural selection, the gardener prunes his shrubs for six main reasons:

1. To increase the output of flowers. This is achieved by encouraging the growth only of the most promising shoots and sacrificing the weaker ones.
2. To alter a plant's natural shape. This should be done only if the shrub is too big for its site, is spoiling other shrubs, or is impeding passage.
3. To encourage new growths. These usually flower more abundantly than older growths, but you should not needlessly sacrifice older shoots that continue to bear flowers.
4. To remove weak or dead growths. These are not merely unproductive and in the way, but they tend to attract insect pests and disease organisms.

5. To reduce the leaf area of newly transplanted shrubs. This helps to balance the activities of leaves and roots by temporarily lessening the food-producing work of the leaves while the rooting system gets used to its new environment. This is especially important with evergreens.
6. To alter the flowering season. This can be achieved by a system of pruning that either retards or accelerates the normal growth rate. For example, a *Buddleia davidii* is normally pruned hard in March and flowers in August. However, if it is left unpruned it will flower in July, while if pruning is delayed until May it will flower in September.

The following remarks are concerned mainly with pruning to promote healthy growth and to increase flower production. Most shrubs fall into one of two groups: those that flower on the previous year's growth, and those that flower on the current year's growth. Before you can have flowers you must have buds; and the key to successful pruning – *when* to prune – is to know when the buds are made by any given plant. You can greatly improve the flowering performance of your shrubs by using secateurs at the appropriate time. This requires careful observation throughout the year, for every month sees shrubs coming into flower.

Pruning after flowering

In previous chapters I have frequently recommended that certain plants be pruned after flowering. To see what this may involve, let us consider for-

sythia, a popular spring-flowering shrub. Its buds are plump and clearly visible all winter, and they burst into yellow flowers in March and April. The buds were obviously developed by the plant in the previous summer, and so are commonly described as 'flowering on the previous year's wood'. You therefore need to prune forsythia immediately after its flowers are finished to give the plant a chance to make new growths on which to bear flowers in the following spring.

However, a mature forsythia also develops buds on other shoots that may be five years old or more, so it is not a good idea to follow the standard advice to 'cut back hard immediately after flowering', because that would simply produce a thicket of young, watery shoots with few flowers and no elegance. Rather, you should take a good look at the plant immediately after it has flowered and remove all weak shoots – those less than pencil-thick – and others that are broken, diseased, or produce an unbalanced shape. Then remove the oldest shoot right from the base and encourage a strong young shoot to take its place. Since most such shrubs develop five to seven basal growths a year, no shoot in the mature plant should be more than five to seven years old.

Other shrubs which benefit from such *selective* pruning immediately

Buddleia davidii exemplifies the many types of shrub whose growths should be cut back hard in early spring. These beautiful August flowers are carried on shoots that develop as a consequence of pruning in March.

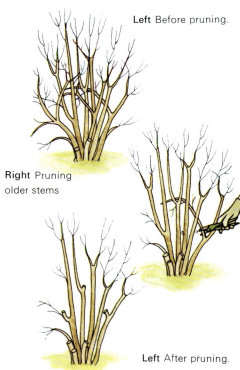

Left Before pruning.

Right Pruning older stems

Left After pruning.

Above Well-established forsythias should have the oldest branches pruned back hard every year. **Left** *Forsythia* × *intermedia*, for instance, is pruned immediately after April flowering to encourage new growths that will flower in the following spring.

after flowering but which flower later in the year include:

> *Deutzia* spp.
> *Hydrangea macrophylla*
> *Philadelphus* spp. (mock orange)
> *Ribes* spp. (flowering currants)
> *Syringa* spp. (lilac)
> *Weigela* spp.

The brooms (*Cytisus* and *Genista* species) also come into this category, but they do not make enough basal growth for a renewal programme. They should be pruned back annually for shape after flowering, but do not cut back into old hard wood or they may die.

There is also a considerable group of shrubs that require *light* pruning immediately after flowering. These shrubs in general are capable of looking after themselves, but they do benefit from the removal of weak growths and the cutting out of straggling or broken boughs. They include species of the following genera:

> *Abelia*
> *Berberis*
> *Chaenomeles*

Camellia
Ceanothus (evergreen spp.)
Chimonanthus
Cistus
Coronilla
Crataegus
Escallonia
Garrya
Hamamelis
Kerria
Pernettya
Spiraea
Ulex
Viburnum

Early-spring pruning

The late-summer- and autumn-flowering shrubs that make their buds at the end of the current summer's growth should be pruned *hard* in early spring. If you grow roses you will know that, after you have cut them back hard in

March, they produce young shoots which flower brilliantly on their tips in June and July. The general method with this group of shrubs is to prune in March or April just as growth commences, cutting back the previous year's flowering shoots to within one or two buds of the older wood and removing any thin, weak, or straggly shoots. Strong young shoots should emerge with late summer flowers. Shrubs in this group include:

Buddleia davidii
Caryopteris spp.
Ceanothus (deciduous spp.)
Fuchsia (hardy spp.)
Hydrangea paniculata
Sambucus spp.
Spartium junceum
Spiraea × bumalda 'Anthony Waterer'
Tamarix spp.

There remains a group of plants valued in gardens not for their flowers but for the winter beauty of their stems. Such colour is always strongest on young shoots, so it is best to cut the whole plant hard back to almost its base in March. Typical examples of such shrubs are:

Cornus spp. (dogwood)
Weigela florida 'Variegata'
Salix spp.
Rubus (white-stemmed brambles)
Stephanandra spp.

Such are the main principles of pruning for flowering and stem growth, but I strongly recommend that you treat them only as a guide and modify them in the light of experience.

Deutzia × rosea needs to be pruned selectively in the summer (see text) to produce this delightful abundance of blossom.

Viburnum tomentosum 'Mariesii'. The viburnums are among many shrubs that benefit from light pruning. For the best results, remove weak or straggly growths immediately after the plants have finished flowering in May or June.

No two gardens are exactly alike and no two shrubs of the same species behave exactly similarly. If you have shrubs of any genus not mentioned above, it probably requires little pruning other than the removal of weak or straggling growths.

Many guides to pruning refer to a 'leading shoot' or simply 'the leader'. Shrubs which are naturally rotund in shape, such as *Thuja* 'Rheingold', or are naturally prostrate, such as *Juniperus procumbens*, do not have a leading shoot; but in most cases a plant's natural direction of growth is upward. In such plants one shoot (the leader) at the growing point dominates all others and soon the characteristic of, say, a columnar cypress is plain for all to see. However, accidents sometimes hap-

pen: a bird too large to be supported may settle on the tip and break it, or snow causes a fracture, or clumsily wielded secateurs snip it off. It is therefore a good idea during the winter to spend time looking over all your shrubs to check whether or not the leading shoots are in fact still leading. Where there is any doubt, leave only the stronger and healthier shoots.

Propagation

I have yet to meet the experienced gardener who does not take a special delight in producing his own new young plants. In its simple forms, propagation is not difficult. The following are the most common methods.

Spanish broom, *Spartium junceum*, is another of the shrubs that produces flowers on the current year's growth. If pruned hard in March it produces strong young shoots that will bear flowers in mid- and late summer.

Layering

Layering simply involves bending down a branch of a shrub in your own border and burying a part near the end of the branch under the soil, so that roots will form there. Several months later the rooted branch is cut away from the parent – and you have a new, well-rooted plant that may be worth several pounds and can make a most welcome gift if it is not needed in your own garden.

It is usual to layer both deciduous and evergreen shrubs in the autumn, although evergreens may also be layered in the spring. Take care to select a suitable branch: it should be one to three years old and must be supple enough to be bent down so that a section about half a metre (1½ ft) from the end can be buried in a vacant area of soil. Having marked the spot for the layer point, dig over the immediate area and work in sand and peat to aid rooting, but avoid making the soil spongy or it may be difficult to fix the branch firmly. Dig out a small hole about 100 mm (4 in) deep. The only equipment you need is a piece of very stout wire about 3 mm (⅛ in) thick that you can bend into a peg with a stem 300 mm (1 ft) long and with a 50 mm (2 in) bend at the top which can be used to hold the shoot down. Alternatively, a wooden peg made from tree prunings will do the job.

Bend the branch down to your prepared soil, then turn up the final 500 mm (1½ ft) so as to form an elbow joint (a 90° angle) that can be secured about 100 mm (4 in) below ground. Before planting, make a slight cut on the outer angle of the joint and scrape off some of the bark. This will interrupt the flow of sap and encourage roots to form; root growth will be further encouraged if you dust the cut with a hormone rooting powder. Put the branch back in the elbow position and hammer in the wire hook to hold it firm. Then put in a stout cane and tie the shoot tip to it – it is all too easy to **forget where your layers are without** such a marker; moreover, the cane will provide support for the new plant. Put the soil back and tread it down firmly. Some easy-rooting plants such as forsythia or kerria will be ready to move in a year; others, such as magnolias, rhododendrons, and camellias may need two years.

Cold-frame cuttings: remove the basal leaves from the selected shoot.

Plant cuttings around edge of well-drained clay pot filled with sandy soil.

Cover pot with plastic bag; hold pot firmly while sealing bag with rubber band.

After labelling, place the pot in a cold frame with the lights shut tight.

Hard-wood cuttings

This method is just as easy as layering but can be used only with a small number of shrubs. Very often the cuttings can be made from prunings; pieces about 300 mm (1 ft) long and fairly robust are the most suitable. Cut them with secateurs square below a bud at the bottom and on a slant above a bud at the top (the different cut angles are merely to help you identify the top and bottom of the cutting when you plant it). Select a patch of light soil, or make it light by forking in sand. Push in a spade to its full depth and rock it to and fro to form a V-shaped nick, into which you push the cuttings. Multiple plantings should be made with the cuttings 80 mm (3 in) apart and in rows 300 mm (1 ft) apart. Bury about two thirds of each cutting and firm the soil with the foot. Hard wood cuttings can be planted from early autumn to Christmas; they will be well rooted after a year, when you can dig them up carefully and plant them in their permanent sites. Shrubs suitable for propagating by this method include:

Buddleia davidii
Cornus spp.
Sambucus spp.
Ligustrum spp.
Ribes spp.
Roses (vigorous types)
Salix spp.
Spiraea × vanhoutei
Tamarix spp.

Cold-frame cuttings

If a greenhouse is not available, you can root many shrubs from cuttings in a cold frame. Suitable cuttings are small shoots about 80 mm (3 in) long, taken during the period around August–October when the base of the shoots has turned pale brown. Pull away the selected shoot so that it brings with it a small portion of the main stem. This is called a 'heel'; if you trim it so that no ragged edges are left, it will resist decay and increase the chances of rooting. The basal leaves should be removed to reduce water loss before the roots have formed and to eliminate a possible source of decay.

If you are unable to obtain a cutting with a 'heel', take your cutting at the junction of this year's and last year's growth; it usually shows itself by a change in colour from a darkish brown to a lighter one. Make a clean cut immediately below a bud and dip the bottom inch in a hormone rooting powder.

Plant your cuttings in a well-drained clay pot filled with sandy soil. Make holes for them at 40 mm ($1\frac{1}{2}$ in) intervals close to the edge of the pot with a dibber or old pencil, and firm the soil around them once they have been inserted. A 90 mm ($3\frac{1}{2}$ in) clay pot will hold five or six cuttings. (Plastic pots can be used but they are

not so good, possibly because the sides are impervious to air.) Water the cuttings thoroughly. Place a plastic bag over the pot, securing it in position with a rubber band, and tuck the open end under the pot to give as airtight a seal as possible. Label the pot, including the species, hybrid, cultivar, or whatever, and the date of planting. Most shrubs root very well in this hermetic atmosphere because water losses from the leaves are kept to a minimum while the new roots are forming. The covered pots should be placed in the cold frame and the lights shut tight. A very light coat of whitewash or proprietary shading on the glass will guard the cuttings against excessive heat from the sun.

There will be no need to attend to the cuttings for several months except to remove any leaves that have fallen from deciduous cuttings. In the warmer weather of spring the plastic bags can be removed from the pots, but the frame should be kept closed until growth is seen from the tips of the cuttings. When they are well rooted, pot on those cuttings with brittle roots (for instance, *Cytisus* and *Genista* spec-

ies); the remainder can be planted out in nursery rows or potted, whichever is more convenient.

Shrubs that can most easily be rooted by this method include deciduous and evergreen barberries, cytisus, cotoneasters, viburnums, and most of the conifers.

Tools

You need only two tools to propagate cuttings – a knife and a pair of secateurs. It is most important that both are really sharp: the knife must make a clean, precise cut. The blade of a pruning knife is too robust for this purpose; it is best to invest in a high-quality steel single-blade horticultural knife (sometimes called a 'budding knife'), which you can sharpen to a very fine edge. Use it only for taking cuttings. Secateurs also need to cut cleanly and accurately, so never use a pair with a loose head. Always clean these tools after use, so that any disease organisms will not be passed from one set of cuttings to the next.

Choisya ternata soft-wood cuttings being dipped in rooting hormone before potting.

Propagating *Senecio* by semi-hard cuttings: (1) removing basal leaves to reduce loss of water while roots are forming; (2) the cuttings ready for potting. *Senecio* cuttings should be taken in late summer or early autumn.

14 Pests and Diseases

DISAPPOINTING performance by shrubs is more often the fault of the gardener than of his plants. Many of the troubles described in this chapter can be avoided, or mitigated, by good gardening practice: careful preparation and planting; keeping plants away from excessive shade, draughty corners, or dry soils next to house walls; correct pruning methods; proper watering and feeding; and regular inspection.

Nonetheless, even the best and most experienced gardener is faced sooner or later with ailing plants. The following is intended to help you to identify the sources of trouble and to take correct action promptly.

Animal pests

Birds
Some birds – bullfinches are especially culpable – take a seemingly malicious pleasure in nipping out the buds of forsythia, flowering cherries, and other shrubs just before flowering. They can be discouraged by netting (which is ugly), by securing lines of black cotton, or by spraying bird repellent before attacks are expected.

Caterpillars
There is a multitude of different species that cause serious defoliation. Young caterpillars can be controlled by derris, which is harmless biologically except to fish. You may need a more long-term control by an organophosphorus compound such as fenitrothion, which is sold under a variety of brand names.

Capsid bug
This is a very active insect which sucks the sap from young shoots of shrubs such as fuchsias, caryopteris, and spiraeas, causing contorted growth and deformed flowers. Treat capsids with HCH, BHC, or fenitrothion.

Greenfly, blackfly, woolly aphid, adelgid
All these are small, very numerous insects which cause havoc by sucking the plants' sap. Bad attacks may damage the plant tissues to a considerable depth and you will need to make very thorough and repeated sprayings with HCH, malathion, nicotine, or other appropriate chemicals. Greenfly produce a sticky honeydew on which disfiguring black moulds grow freely, and early spraying is most important. Woolly aphids and adelgids (which attack only conifers) produce a protective white waxy 'wool' which should be painted with methylated spirit.

Leaf miner
This does just what its name suggests, burrowing into the leaf tissues and leaving a colourless winding track. It may disfigure holly, euonymus, lilacs, azaleas, and other shrubs with unsightly blisters and trails, but it rarely does serious damage. It can be treated with malathion.

Rhododendron bug
This insect feeds on the lower leaf surfaces, causing mottling and the edges to curl downwards and inwards. It dis-

Above left Capsids suck the sap of shoots of many shrubs. **Above** Leaf miners disfigure foliage with their tell-tale tracks. **Right** Honey fungus fruiting bodies resemble toadstools. The fungus attacks most shrubs and can be checked rather than cured.

The rhododendron bug feeds on leaves.

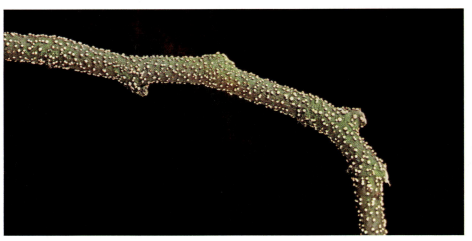

figures rather than harms and may be treated with malathion.

Scale insects

These insects are about 3 mm ($\frac{1}{8}$ in) long and attach themselves to soft stems and leaves; they cover themselves with a hard protective coat and do not move thereafter, feeding by sucking sap. In large numbers they have a debilitating effect on a plant. Yew and willow are each attacked by a particular species of scale; the ubiquitous brown scale attacks almost every type of plant. If present only in small numbers the insects can be wiped away with cotton wool soaked in methylated spirit. Bad infestations should be sprayed with malathion in May.

Fungal and bacterial diseases

Fungi are plants that lack chlorophyll and depend on other plants to provide their food supply. They commonly infect many host plants, especially shrubs, with a variety of lethal or disfiguring diseases, of which the following are typical.

Honey fungus

So called because of the colour of the fruiting bodies, resembling toadstools, which appear in autumn at the base of affected plants, honey fungus attacks anything shrubby. Underground it spreads by characteristic black 'bootlaces'. There is no certain cure for this killer fungus, but various proprietary compounds can help to check it.

Fireblight

Another killer, this bacterium attacks cotoneasters, pyracanthas, and other plants in the Rosaceae family. The symptoms are many brown leaves that look scorched but do not fall off; whole branches die off, and ultimately the entire shrub may die. All infected plants should be burnt at once.

Clematis wilt

This is a disease specific to the genus *Clematis*, and infected plants may suddenly collapse. They should be cut back almost to ground level. Spray new growths with benlate. The wilt is especially prone to attack plants of inherently poor quality, so a basic preventive measure is to buy stock only from a reputable supplier. It will also help if you plant new clematis fairly deep, with the top of the root ball at least 50 mm (2 in) below the surface.

Coral spot

This disease can attack dead as well as living plant tissue. The distinctive raised, coral pink spots are frequently seen on last year's bean sticks, and spores from this and other sources enter wounds in living shrubs. It is rarely a killer but it seriously disfigures shrubs. Burn all dead wood and cut out and burn infected branches. Paint pruning cuts with one of the proprietary compounds available.

Powdery mildew

This white powdery disease is one of the most familiar in the garden. Mahonias, clematis, barberries, and euonymus are among many shrubs that are susceptible, especially in dry weather and when the plants are in poor

Coral spot attacks shrubs at pruning cuts.

health. Remove infected shoots and make at least two applications of benlate spray.

Rhododendron bud blast

This disease is transmitted to a plant by a leafhopper insect while it is feeding. The buds turn brown and may exhibit black bristles, which are part of the fungus. Infected buds, which do not drop, become hard; this distinguishes them from frost-damaged buds, which turn soft. The leafhopper can be killed by spraying infected plants with malathion in late summer.

Rust

Among shrubs this is a disease mainly of barberries. The symptoms are brown pustules that form on the lower leaf surfaces. Foliar feeding with one of the proprietary compounds to improve the plants' health is probably the best preventive measure.

Rhododendron bud blast, due to leafhoppers.

Frost damage can be severe after a mild spell.

Weather problems

There is, of course, little you can do to prevent damage caused by hostile weather conditions, but the following notes may help you to minimize the effects of such damage.

Frost
Frost can damage the blooms of many plants which flower early, such as rhododendrons and camellias. The damage is especially severe if frost follows a mild spell. Tell-tale signs are the flowers and/or buds turning brown; those affected should be removed. Frost can also cause cracks in the bark of large woody shrubs, especially rhododendrons. This is not dangerous in itself, but it may open the way to attack by disease organisms, so clean the cracks and paint them with a proprietary sealing compound.

Drought
The first sign that drought is affecting plants is when the leaves begin to droop. Wilting, as this is called, enables the plant to minimize loss of water. Plants must be watered immediately wilting occurs or the leaves will soon turn brown and drop and the plants may die. If possible, provide the plants with a heavy layer of mulch, as this will prevent water evaporating from the soil.

Spring scorch
This usually occurs in cold weather in early spring. At this time the leaves are producing food but the plants cannot replace the moisture lost in this process because the roots have not yet become fully active after the winter. As a result the leaves begin to droop and will eventually fall. Frequent spraying of the leaves with water is the only possible cure for this condition.

Winter damage
A common symptom of trouble in evergreens in the winter is drying out of the leaf tips. This also arises from a failure of the root system to work normally, which may be due to very heavy frost, waterlogging, or drought. The damage is not usually very serious, but you should remove the affected leaves.

Other problems

Mineral deficiencies
Plants need a balanced 'diet' and one of the commonest reasons for their lack of health is that the soil is deficient in one or more of the mineral elements that plants need, albeit in tiny quantities. Sometimes the wanted mineral may in fact be present but the constitution of the soil is such as to prevent the plant absorbing it (see Chapter 9 and the discussion of chlorosis). The commonest deficiencies can usually be identified by examining the leaves, as follows.
Iron leaves turn yellow between green veins.
Nitrogen leaves in spring or summer assume autumnal tints of red and orange.
Magnesium leaf centres turn brown between the veins.

Potash leaf edges appear scorched. Foliar feeds containing the required minerals will usually make good moderate deficiencies. More serious cases need a sequestrene and a spring dressing of a 'complete' fertilizer (containing nitrate, phosphate, and potash) at a rate of 100 g/m² (4 oz/sq yd).

Weeds
These are as inevitable as they are tiresome and, apart from the important preventive device of using ground cover (see Chapter 9), there are two ways of dealing with them.

HOEING   Use a flat or Dutch hoe when the seedlings are 10 mm ($\frac{1}{2}$ in) or smaller. Hoeing should be done once a fortnight. It is cheap and practical in small gardens.

WEEDKILLERS There are two main types. The first, of which dalapon is typical, destroys the green pigment (chlorophyll) in leaves, so preventing a plant from making food. It is harmless when applied around brown stems and it loses its effect on contact with the soil. Since this type is equally damaging to weeds and cultivated plants, be careful how you apply it. Use a fine-rosed watering can rather than a sprayer, and if possible choose an almost windless day.

Soil-acting weedkillers such as simazine inhibit the growth of weed seedlings among your shrubs. They provide a herbicidal seal in the surface layer of the soil, which should be left undisturbed for as long as possible, and should be applied in February.

Note Bear in mind that weedkillers and pesticides are poisons. Keep all containers out of reach of children and animals; wash all equipment such as watering cans thoroughly after use, and if possible reserve a set of such equipment exclusively for use with these chemicals. Always read and follow the manufacturers' instructions carefully. This will ensure not only that you mix the correct concentrations but also that you avoid using the chemicals on cultivated plants that may be damaged or even killed by them.

15 A Shrub-lover's Calendar

THE list of plants under each month is of species, hybrids, and cultivars that will normally be in flower during the period in question. None of the lists is exhaustive; the intention is simply to indicate the range of form and colour available.

January

Make sure all newly planted shrubs are firmly in the ground and, if necessary, staked; frost and high winds can move even the best-planted shrubs. Remove any dead branches, diseased growths, and plants likely to obstruct paths. Sow very small seeds such as rhododendrons in warmth late this month or next.

Chimonanthus fragrans (winter sweet)
Erica carnea and cultivars (winter-flowering heaths)
Hamamelis mollis (Chinese witch hazel)
Jasminum nudiflorum (winter jasmine)
Lonicera fragrantissima (winter honeysuckle)
Mahonia japonica
Viburnum tinus (laurustinus)

February

Rooted layers of rhododendron, jasmine, forsythia, and others can be carefully dug up, severed from the parent, and planted in their permanent place or given to friends. Now is a good time to plant containers intended for use on patios or terraces. Hedges which have grown thin at the base should be cut hard back to about 300 mm (1 ft) to encourage them to break again.

Cornus mas (cornelian cherry)
Daphne mezereum (mezereon)
Erica carnea and cultivars
Garrya elliptica (tassel bush)
Hamamelis vernalis (Ozark witch hazel)
Jasminum nudiflorum (winter-flowering jasmine)
Mahonia japonica
Viburnum × bodnantense

March

Many shrubs layer well at this season, notably lilac and chimonanthus. Prune the late-summer-flowering shrubs such as *Buddleia davidii*, *Ceanothus* 'Gloire de Versailles', caryopteris, *Spiraea × bumalda*, and hardy fuchsias and also shrubs with attractive bark – cornus, willows, and others. *Clematis × jackmanii*, *C. viticella*, and their cultivars must be pruned hard back to 300 mm (1 ft).

Camellia japonica
Chaenomeles speciosa (japonica)
Corylopsis pauciflora
Erica mediterranea
Forsythia × intermedia
Garrya elliptica
Hamamelis japonica (witch hazel)
Magnolia stellata
Mahonia aquifolium (Oregon grape)
Rhododendron hybrids

April

Layer magnolias and hamamelis. Prune forsythias and other early flowers to allow maximum flowering wood growth to develop by next spring. Keep a sharp look out for evidence of chlorosis, especially on alkaline soils, and apply a sequestrene compound at the first signs. Sow stratified barberry seeds out of doors. Towards the end of the month, transplant evergreens.

Amelanchier lamarckii (snowy mespilus)
Berberis darwinii
Camellia japonica
Cytisus spp.
Kerria japonica
Magnolia salicifolia
Pieris floribunda
Rhododendron hybrids
Ribes sanguineum (flowering currant)
Spiraea × arguta

Above left *Ceanothus × veitchianus* flowers in May or June. **Right** *Cornus mas* blooms in February or March.

May

Prune forsythia, *Prunus triloba*, kerria, and similar early-flowering shrubs. Remove dead wood (now clearly visible) and weak shoots. Pot on rooted root cuttings. Watch out for leaf-eating caterpillars and aphids, and spray them before the infestation becomes serious. Powdery mildew can appear in any summer month: spray it with benlate at first signs.

Azalea hybrids
Buddleia globosa
Camellia japonica
Ceanothus spp.
Choisya ternata (Mexican orange blossom)
Cistus spp.
Clematis montana
Enkianthus spp.
Genista spp.
Halesia carolina (snowdrop tree)
Magnolia × soulangeana (yulan)
Pernettya spp.
Pieris spp.
Potentilla spp. (shrubby cinquefoil)
Rhododendron spp.
Rosa spp.
Wisteria sinensis

June

Take your earliest soft-wood cuttings of fuchsias, deutzias, and philadelphus if a heated frame or similar is available. Hedges producing shoots rapidly – *Lonicera nitida*, *L.* 'Yunnan', and privet are typical – can be given their first clipping, as can thujas and yews. Prune *Clematis florida*, *C. lanuginosa*, and *C. patens* and cultivars by shortening old growths immediately after flowering.

Abelia triflora
Berberis darwinii
Cistus spp. (sun roses)
Deutzia spp.
Genista spp.
Kalmia latifolia (calico bush)
Philadelphus spp. and cultivars
Rhododendron spp.
Rosa spp.
Spartium junceum (Spanish broom)
Syringa spp. and cultivars (lilacs)
Weigela spp.

July

This is the month to take semi-hard wood cuttings. The base of such cuttings will be turning brown and can remain alive longer while roots are forming; the cuttings can be rooted in cold frames. Cistus, ceanothus, escallonias, hydrangeas, potentillas, and pyracanthas are among many which are suited to this method. Remove dead heads from lilacs, azaleas, and rhododendrons to avoid the strain of seed formation. Clip holly hedges.

Buddleia davidii (butterfly bush)
Calluna vulgaris and cultivars (heather)
Escallonia spp.
Fuchsia spp. and cultivars
Hebe spp. and cultivars (veronicas)
Hydrangea spp.
Hypericum spp. and cultivars
Lavandula spica (lavender)
Olearia spp.
Philadelphus cultivars

August

The last of the deciduous semi-hard wood cuttings should be taken now. This is an important month for hedge clipping. The quicker soft-growth hedges such as loniceras and privet need their second clip. Beech and hornbeam should be clipped now if you want them to retain their leaves all winter in their autumn colours. Remove green shoots from variegated plants.

Caryopteris × clandonensis
Ceratostigma willmottianum
Daboecia cantabrica (St Daboec's heath)
Genista tinctoria (dyer's greenweed)
Hibiscus syriacus (shrubby mallow)
Indigofera spp.
Hydrangea spp. and cultivars
Potentilla spp. and cultivars

Hibiscus syriacus 'Blue Bird', one of the most attractive of the late-flowering deciduous shrubs, is at its best in August.

November

Continue planting new arrivals. Protect tender shrubs such as fuchsias with a mound of coarse grit over the crown; myrtles, ceanothus, abutilons, and others welcome a covering of dry bracken. Take hard-wood cuttings of cornus, willows, *Buddleia davidii*, and others.
Calluna vulgaris
Erica carnea
Jasminum nudiflorum
Lonicera standishii (winter honey-suckle)
Mahonia × media
Viburnum farreri
Prunus subhirtella 'Autumnalis' (autumn cherry)
Colourful fruits can be enjoyed this month on shrubs of the following genera:
Amelanchier
Aucuba
Berberis
Chaenomeles
Cotoneaster
Crataegus
Euonymus
Pernettya
Symphoricarpos (snowberry)
Viburnum

September

Take semi-hard cuttings of evergreens such as holly, aucubas, thujas, chamae-cyparis, and laurels. Although April is the best month to move evergreens, they can be successfully planted now before the soil temperature drops.
Abelia chinensis
Aralia elata (Japanese angelica tree)
Clematis jackmanii
Clerodendrum bungei
Colutea arborescens (bladder senna)
Fuchsia cultivars
Hibiscus spp.
Hydrangea spp. and cultivars
Leycesteria formosa
Passiflora (passion flower)
Perovskia atriplicifolia (Russian sage)
Romneya coulteri (tree poppy)

Fuchsia 'Mme Cornelissen', with its delightful semi-double blooms, is one of many fuchsia hybrids that flower well into the autumn.

October

This is the time to re-site shrubs already in the garden to create more space: new shrubs will be arriving from the nurseryman and should be planted immediately they arrive. Layer hamamelis, kerrias, and other suitable shrubs. Collect and stratify (mix with moist sand) seeds of barberries, cotoneasters, and others, and stand them under a north wall for six months to a year (the period depends on the toughness of the seed coats, which varies from species to species).
Calluna vulgaris (heathers)
Ceratostigma willmottianum
Erica carnea
Erica vagans (Cornish heath)
Fatsia japonica
Fuchsia spp.
Hydrangea spp. and cultivars
Mahonia × media
Potentilla spp.

December

Never plant in frosty weather or when the soil is excessively wet. If you are still awaiting arrival of new plants it is advisable to take out a trench, and then to heel in the plants when they arrive to await better planting weather. Check all shrub labels and renew those that are becoming illegible.
Erica carnea
Erica darleyensis
Hamamelis mollis
Jasminum nudiflorum
Lonicera fragrantissima
Mahonia × media
Viburnum × bodnantense
Viburnum tinus
Colourful fruits can be enjoyed this month on the following genera:
Arbutus
Ilex
Pyracantha
Skimmia

Index

Acknowledgments

The publishers would like to thank the following organisations and individuals for their kind permission to reproduce the photographs in this book:

Heather Angel 9; A–Z Botanical Collection Limited 1, 14, 15, 23 above left, 65 below right, 66, 71, 75, 78 above left, 84, 94; Pat Brindley 30, 44 above right, 47, 53 above right, 63, 78 below left, 79 below right, 81, 85, 89; Bruce Colman Limited 21, 26 below right, 39, 82; Valerie Finnis 27, 35, 40 below left, 48; Brian Furner 40 above left; John Harris 87 centre and left and below right; George Hyde 23 below right, 65 above right; Leslie Johns and Associates 46 above left; M. A. Knight 77; Natural History Photographic Agency 50, 61 below left; Natural Science Photos 29, 41, 52, 92; Royal Horticultural Society's Garden, Wisley 88 centre and above left, 90 above left and right and below right, 91; Harry Smith Horticultural Photographic Collection 2, 5, 10, 11, 12, 13, 16, 19, 20, 22, 23 above right, 24, 25 above and below right, 26 above left, 31, 32, 33, 34, 36, 37, 46 below left, 49, 51, 53 below right, 54, 55, 56 above and below right, 57, 59, 60 above and below right, 61 above left, 64 above and below left, 69 above right, 73 above and below right, 74, 79 above right, 83, 93, 95; John Topham Picture Library 38; Michael Warren 7, 42, 43, 44 below right, 45, 67